GOD'S
HEALING POWER

GOD'S
HEALING POWER

FINDING YOUR TRUE SELF
THROUGH MEDITATION

B.K. JAYANTI

STERLING ETHOS
An imprint of Sterling Publishing Co., Inc.

New York / London
www.sterlingpublishing.com

STERLING and the distinctive Sterling logo are registered trademarks of
Sterling Publishing Co., Inc.

Library of Congress Cataloging-in-Publication Data

Jayanti, B. K.
  God's healing power : finding your true self through meditation / B.K. Jayanti.
     p. cm.
  ISBN 978-1-4027-6639-8
  1. Meditation—Brahmakumari. 2. Brahmakumari—Doctrines. I. Title.
  BL1274.255.J37 2010
  294.5'436—dc22

                                                                    2009053399

10 9 8 7 6 5 4 3 2 1

Published by Sterling Publishing Co., Inc.
387 Park Avenue South, New York, NY 10016
Originally published in 2002 by Penguin Group, New York; subsequently published
  in 2006 by Brahma Kumaris Information Services Ltd., London
© 2006 Brahma Kumaris Information Services Ltd .
Distributed in Canada by Sterling Publishing
^{c}/o Canadian Manda Group, 165 Dufferin Street
Toronto, Ontario, Canada M6K 3H6
Distributed in the United Kingdom by GMC Distribution Services
Castle Place, 166 High Street, Lewes, East Sussex, England BN7 1XU
Distributed in Australia by Capricorn Link (Australia) Pty. Ltd.
P.O. Box 704, Windsor, NSW 2756, Australia

Sterling ISBN 978-1-4027-6639-8

For information about custom editions, special sales, premium and
corporate purchases, please contact Sterling Special Sales
Department at 800-805-5489 or specialsales@sterlingpublishing.com.

CONTENTS

INTRODUCTION

Meditation is a natural state of being. Consciously or not, we all experience meditative states from time to time.

The moments when we enjoy our own company, in solitude; when we are pulled into what we might call daydreaming; when we are absorbed in watching nature's beauty—these are all forms of meditation. The times when we awaken with joy, celebrating the gift of life, or before we fall asleep, feeling cared for, secure, comfortable, and protected. Or when it is raining outside, we are warm and cozy on the inside, and the heart feels gratitude—these also are expressions of meditation. When we hear music and our hearts soar with love and we feel uplifted, that too is a sense of meditation.

The insights in this book describe a more formal and focused approach to meditation than daydreaming or listening to music, but it is still a natural process. The aim is that through understanding, the process should be brought under conscious control so that deeper and potentially life-transforming experiences become systematically available.

There is a need for this focus, because today, for so much of the time, materialism traps our minds.

Earning, spending, and acquiring are all necessary to sustain life, but when they become everything to us, selfishness intensifies and the spirit atrophies. We may then feel that this is how human life has always been and will continue to be, but that need not be so. Meditation nourishes the soul as food nourishes the body. It is vital for each one of us. The journey of life is necessarily a challenge, with obstacles along the way, but it passes more comfortably and constructively when the path of meditation is understood. The journey may be similar, but the experience becomes different. Meditation increases our ability to travel with balance, stability, and peace, much as a good set of tires improves comfort and safety on the roads.

If we are to be successful in meditation, we need the right technique for our particular purposes. Many just want to learn to relax, and there are certainly a number of techniques available in the marketplace that will help people learn how to do that.

Others are looking for greater control over their minds and want to improve their powers of concentration. A popular technique is mantra meditation, in which one is given a holy word or sacred sound for chanting either out loud or silently within the mind. Concentrating in this way can bring feelings of deep peace and contentment. Also, while focusing on the mantra, the mind doesn't have space to run elsewhere, and so worries and anxieties recede.

Meditating on scenes of nature—a sunset, a sunrise, a tree, a beautiful vista—is another means of nourishing the soul. Almost any aspect of nature can bring us back to a point of calmness and peace because of the beauty and truth nature contains. This beauty soothes and uplifts, and the mind's fears and troubles diminish. We feel stronger and more in touch with reality.

RAJA YOGA

Raja Yoga meditation, which underpins the insights shared in this book, is a powerful method for connecting to the positive, nurturing, loving, and strengthening inner aspects of life. The highest source of this inner nourishment is God, and every human soul, as a child of God, has a right to a direct relationship with its parent. The prophets and messengers who founded the great religious traditions indicated that all souls can have this relationship with the Supreme, and the time has now come for us to reclaim that right. The world needs us to do this!

Meditation, accurately directed, makes God accessible to everyone. With meditation, we become better able to make choices that we feel happy with the next day, or the next week, or ten years later. So often on the journey of life, we come to a crossroads and make choices that with hindsight may not be seen as wise. The bumps and twists that follow may be with us long afterward. And yes, we may learn from them as we live with the results of our decisions. But especially in today's condition, when it is difficult to know what the future holds or where it may lie, our choices carry more significance than ever. Our decisions require not only logic and reason but also an appreciation of truth and a sense of intuition.

Raja Yoga meditation is simple in that it doesn't require a mantra, chanting, special postures, or external scenes of beauty. It does, however, have a high aim: becoming self-sovereign, master of the mind and senses. It teaches that there is a natural royalty in us that is capable of bringing strength and beauty into our relationships and behavior. This royalty emerges when we renew our awareness of the inner self, the essence of our being, in relationship with the Supreme.

Raja Yoga offers a meditation that we can carry inside ourselves so that we can practice it not just when we're sitting quietly but also as we continue to fulfill our daily tasks and responsibilities.

It allows each of us to get to know God and to love God so that it remains easy for us to remember God no matter what else we may be doing, as lovers remember each other however far apart they may be. The goal is to be able to exercise such a power of choice over our thoughts and feelings as to bring a positive response into any situation, no matter how bad or sad that situation might seem. In a world beset with difficulties, the positivity generated by this creative use of the mind gives our hearts the strength to cope. Amazingly, the feelings of worry, anger, fear, and hopelessness that dominate many people's lives come to be seen as unnecessary, and hanging on to them is seen as part of the problem. To let go of those negative habits of mind and embrace God's positive energy becomes a solution in itself.

I'll be describing how in Raja Yoga we turn our attention inward in order to come to the awareness of our spiritual identity and link the mind with the Supreme. In this way, we encounter the beauty of our own inner being and find ourselves drawn more and more to the truth within. Meditation enables us to discover the eternal relationship we had forgotten or perhaps conveniently ignored when our thoughts were absorbed in the world of the physical senses.

As we will see, the inner journey starts with a very simple step: visualizing the essence of the self as a tiny star situated between the eyes at the center of the forehead. This is the "I" within who thinks, feels, dreams, understands, interprets, and responds to the physical world around a person. An analogy is a miner's lamp, but whereas that is still a physical object, external to its owner, with this light of inner awareness, the light of I, the soul radiates from a dimensionless point. When I allow my consciousness to rest in this awareness and identity of being a point of light, I become able to let go of thoughts and feelings concerning the body and its activities and relationships. No longer pulled this way and that by the flux of events, I feel better able to be myself.

Even moments like this are very refreshing. Yoga means "union," and when attention goes inside in this way, a memory begins to stir of a deep connectedness to all of life lying behind the physical differences. Mundane concerns lose significance, mental noise is reduced, and our higher nature emerges. This is nourished most powerfully by the feeling and awareness that we are one family of humanity, offspring of a Supreme Parent or Seed, the One who has been known as God.

In Raja Yoga meditation, as with the self, God is visualized as a star, a singular source of consciousness, nonphysical and eternal. However, whereas the natural wisdom and goodness of human beings has often become depleted, this One is understood and experienced as being totally giving, radiating a divine light that is like an energy of truth.

In meditation, the experience is of the light coming from above, as from the sun, although it is not a matter of physical dimensions. When I become introspective, see myself as a being of light, become aware of the Supreme Light, and allow myself to become absorbed in that light, truth returns into my own being.

When we are overinvolved in the physical world, whose nature is one of constant change, our thoughts and feelings are always on the move and the mind can never be at rest. The ability to create moments of calm brings us back to the gentler, generous side of the human personality, which the harshness of today's world tends to make us neglect or forget. Peace, calm, and strength of mind are also essential for physical health in a world where the potential for stress and burnout is everywhere.

In today's frenetic times, when we have so often forgotten to take care of either mind or body, meditation is a means of enabling God's healing power to restore us to wholeness. In silence, as we connect and commune with the Divine, God's light and love reach the soul and the pains and wounds we are carrying begin to heal. This inner focus relieves us from the sorrow that has arisen through our relationships and circumstances.

As the soul appreciates once more its own inner wealth and goodness, the body also reaps fruits from this process, gaining strength that was being drained away by suffering. Medical treatment, when needed, works better and patients recover faster. When sickness or old age makes a body uninhabitable, the soul is much more likely to be able to leave with ease and even happiness than it can when consciousness is locked into the outer, physical identity.

Raja Yoga meditation makes us free by increasing our inner strength. It can be practiced any time, any place, anywhere. We can do it alone or in a large gathering. We can meditate without any artificial postures, chanting, or expensive courses.

The path of meditation does not have to cut us off from others, as some believe. Instead, by liberating us from negative influences, it increases our ability to be ourselves and to serve and cooperate with others. It enables us to draw on God's love and wisdom. It opens up our understanding and perception so that we begin to take charge of our feelings, emotions, and future.

Meditation is not difficult, and it costs nothing. All it requires is our intention—our will. If we are willing to learn to meditate, to understand a few basic concepts, and to give the time and commitment to practicing them, our lives will be transformed in a very natural and simple way.

The book is divided into four parts: The Soul, God, Relationships, and The Destination. The aim is that if you read it sequentially, the book will take you on a journey of rediscovery, bringing you back to an awareness of your original strength and beauty.

Within the four sections, nuggets of understanding or insight are presented, along with suggested trains of thought that may help in your meditation. I hope that by opening the book at random from time to time and dipping into the contents, you will find useful spiritual support for your journey.

1 | THE SOUL

MIND AND MATTER

KNOWING MYSELF

Meditation means focusing my attention on aspects of eternal truth. When I am able to listen, eternity speaks to me from a multitude of sources.

Sitting alone beside the sea, it's easy to feel transported by the vast energy of the wind and the waves into a realm beyond limitations of time and space. When I contemplate the beauty and complexity of a flower, my sense of wonder over creation is rekindled. Gazing at the stars on a still night, I feel drawn out of my body into the immensity of the cosmos. Nature's awesome power mirrors the vastness of my own eternal identity. Understanding and experiencing that identity is the secret to being able to meditate at will.

POWER OF THE MIND

Matter has its own limits. It's fixed in time and space. Mind, however, is beyond limits in terms of physical parameters.

When I begin to look at what is going on in my mind, its amazing power is apparent. It can link me to a friend in New York or Bombay in a fraction of a second. I can think about yesterday or about twenty years ago, about tonight or the next five years. My mind can even move in a dozen different directions at once.

Thoughts themselves have different levels of power. Sometimes they flit past, leaving hardly a trace. At other times they are accompanied by such feelings as to influence my entire outlook as well as my inner state of being. Thinking about a successful holiday I had last summer, for example, I could find myself carried back into that beautiful experience. Filled with warmth and happiness, I will radiate this to others nearby. By contrast, thoughts about the death of my best friend ten years ago will have a very different impact.

CHANGING THE PATTERN

The energy of thought and feeling is not a physical energy. It is extremely subtle. It transcends the limits of matter. Yet it is closely connected with the body and requires the body for its expression. Some scientists call it an energy of consciousness.

I have to channel and discipline this energy if I want to meditate. In fact, one of my main reasons for wanting to meditate could be the need to discipline this energy, which is at the heart of my identity and my life. Day and night, for as long as I have lived, it has kept going and going. But when I haven't taken care of it, it sometimes has gone off in a wrong direction.

When my thoughts and feelings are disorganized, my life will be unstable and my relationships and health will tend to be so, too. Worse still, if I don't know what is going on in my mind, I may end up being my own worst enemy, sabotaging opportunities for finding happiness that come my way.

Often, the memories my thoughts bring up have been of suffering. Sometimes I have found myself reliving that suffering repeatedly even though I know this leaves me feeling drained. I want to change that pattern.

THE SPIRIT WITHIN

As the first step in meditation, I give myself the luxury of looking at what is going on inside me at a deeper level. I don't want to be a stranger to myself any longer but to know myself, value myself, respect myself, and even love myself. I want to learn to use my thoughts in the most effective way possible. I want to make my mind my friend.

I decide to find a place where I can sit for a few minutes without interruptions in order to focus on the self and explore my inner world. Am I just a product of chemical and electrical activity in the brain, as is commonly believed in recent times? Scientists have learned much about the mechanics of our physical functioning, but most admit that the qualitative experience of being alive remains a mystery.

From a spiritual perspective, there has also been some confusion, with many different schools of thought about what the mind or soul is and how it works. This has been true even among Eastern philosophies, which historically have given much attention to this question.

In meditation, a simple yet powerful way of thinking, to clarify who I am is to understand that although my body is essential to my experience of life, it is not me. In the teachings of Raja Yoga, soul and body are considered separate entities no matter what parallels or connections there ultimately may be between them. The mind, which gives rise to my thoughts and feelings, is seen as a faculty of the soul, not of the body.

It is like the difference between a television set and the programs received through that set. The programs originate in the minds of the producers, not in the television set itself. So it is with my own thoughts. They originate in a spiritual dimension of being, in consciousness, not in the brain. When I realize this and really understand this distinction, it is very empowering. Just as I need to be discriminating in my TV viewing, I can learn to make choices between thoughts and feelings that are useful and uplifting for myself and others and those which bring me down.

I AM A STAR

I am a soul, and I have a body. I am nonphysical and eternal, with a capacity for transcending the limitations of the physical world. I express myself in different ways through my body, but I exist in my own right.

To experience this distinction, it is useful to visualize I, the soul, as a pinpoint of radiant light, like a star, situated behind the eyes in the center of the forehead. Let's try this:

> *Turning my attention within, I select one thought,*
> *concerning my own identity . . . I see myself*
> *not in physical terms but as that inner being, of*
> *light . . . I just practice this visualization, creating*
> *an image of a point of light, powerful, concentrated, in*
> *the center of the forehead . . . I hold this image in my*
> *mind . . . other thoughts are there, but for the moment*
> *this is the thought I am interested in, and I hold it in*
> *my awareness . . . As I continue to focus on this point*
> *of light, I can feel the consciousness of my physical*
> *form fade away . . . and I begin to touch my own*
> *inner qualities . . . I am this light . . . I am this*
> *truth . . . I discover peace, strength and goodness within*

myself . . . and the feeling grows that my heart has been blocked for a while, but now there's a melting taking place. Defenses that I had been putting up are beginning to come down . . . and I recognize the love that exists within me.

B. K.
JAYANTI

8

CHARGING THE BATTERY

My thoughts are my own creation. If I choose, I can let the awareness of the body recede and guide my thoughts into an awareness of my eternal identity.

Using the power of my mind, I access qualities of peace and positivity within my being that are original to my nature but that become concealed by limited, overly materialistic ways of thinking and behaving.

I rediscover benevolent feelings—a natural goodwill—linked with those positive qualities. The feelings in turn influence my behavior in a positive way—the stronger the experience, the greater the effect. As both my mind and my body become charged, like a battery, with this positive power, a natural radiance of love and happiness develops.

Furthermore, my behavior influences my meditation. If I act in ways that are in line with my inner qualities, with my true self, I am able to experience those qualities easily as and when I choose.

Gradually, as I become confident enough to let go of selfish tendencies and wise enough to recognize and understand those tendencies in others, I learn how to remain constantly true to myself while engaged in actions and relationships, as well as in meditation.

THOUGHTS AND ACTIONS

Meditation and life are intertwined. It is not possible to separate them. As is the quality of my thoughts, so will be my actions, and the quality of my actions feeds back into my thoughts.

When I really understand this, it becomes clear that the right way to live is to marry both of these sides within my life and to do this here and now.

Actions performed according to a selfish consciousness, without love, have led to a meaningless existence, causing feelings of pain and emptiness in many hearts. However, devotional or meditation practices performed in isolation and not reflected in actions have resulted in spirituality that is divorced from reality and is unable to influence life in the right way.

I want my consciousness to become such that I can draw on the richness of a life of engagement and involvement in the world but one fueled with the energy and spiritual power that meditation can provide.

DEVELOPING SOUL-CONSCIOUSNESS

When I consider myself a soul inhabiting a body, the consequences are doubly empowering.

In meditation, in accessing the pure consciousness of the soul, there is joy. Detached from the body, traveling into myself, beyond the realms of the physical and into a dimension where there is absolute stillness, I feel deeply connected with the divine. Through such an experience, it is as though every part of my being becomes refreshed. But I have a life to be lived here and now, and so I need to learn how to maintain soul-consciousness while performing everyday actions. This practice is perhaps more urgently needed now than ever before. It becomes a means of taking charge of my thoughts, feelings, and physical senses. Loss of this control resulting from loss of a sense of distinction between body and soul has been responsible for much distress.

THE DRIVER AND THE CAR

A variety of images help strengthen the awareness that I, the soul, am different from this physical body.

One is of the driver and the car. Being a good driver requires 100 percent alertness and an ability to use the accelerator, brakes, gears, and steering wheel with precision in order to be fully in control of the vehicle and avoid collisions.

In the same way, as I move through life, I need to keep my mental and physical faculties in order. If I use my thoughts and senses in the right way, they will serve me well and take me where I choose. If I let them take over, however, accidents are liable to occur.

When I am aware of myself as a soul and of my body as a vehicle through which to experience life, I am in a much better position to dictate the nature of my experiences than I am when I identify with my body.

For example, looking out through my eyes, I don't have to take in all the images and information along the way. I can choose to absorb what is useful for me and not register distracting images. My journey is going to pass more safely this way, compared with when my senses are constantly pulled in different directions.

I want to use my senses positively, as their master, so that they will help instill in me a fulfilled and giving frame of mind, leading me toward goodness, truth, and harmony rather than self-indulgence and conflict. Then the risk of colliding with other people will be reduced.

I see the innocence on a child's face. I see the beauty in a patch of blue amid dark clouds. I see the pure dewdrop glistening on a blade of grass. I see and understand situations, too—it would be dangerous to ignore them—but I look for the positive in them, and so I am not deflected from my goal.

I, as the driver in charge of this vehicle, the body, also learn to monitor the feelings that are transmitted outward through my eyes and my words. When these feelings stay positive, filled with consideration and respect, that too helps ensure that my journey passes smoothly and enjoyably.

When I stay alert, conscious, and aware like this, my actions bring me closer to my truth and I am able to share my goodness with others around me. When I lose awareness for even a moment, there is danger. If bad feeling erupts and ill will is expressed, time and energy are lost.

Sitting quietly, I visualize my eternal identity, the being of light, the spark of awareness, of consciousness, in the

*center of my forehead . . . I realize that I am the being
in charge of this physical vehicle, the body . . . I am
the being that has awareness . . . I create the thought of
peace in my mind, knowing this to be my own natural
state, and I allow this thought to reach deep within me so
that I touch into the peace . . . and as I look out into the
world, I share this peace . . . through my eyes, I send
out rays of peace and light . . . I, the driver of this
vehicle, in the awareness of being the master of my senses,
resolve that the words I speak will be of goodness and
peace . . . that the actions I perform will share the peace I
am experiencing.*

ACTOR ON THE STAGE

As well as learning to distinguish between my self and my body, I need to understand that there is a difference between who I really am and the role or roles I am currently playing.

An actor, even in the middle of the most dramatic scenes, even while crying or laughing or shouting, knows he is not the part itself. He knows he is something more than that and that when the play is over, he won't cease to exist.

There is great strength for me if in the same way, while playing different roles on the stage of the world, I hold on to the inner awareness of my eternal identity as the being of pure consciousness—of peace, of truth, of light, of love.

Separating role and actor increases opportunities for seeing what my role actually demands and reduces the chances of being unduly influenced by others. If I'm able to protect my inner identity, it is also much easier for me to switch roles. If I lose myself in a particular role, I am not able to see beyond immediate needs.

As a mother, for example, I may also be called upon to play the role of wife, career woman, community worker, or friend. I'll have a better chance of being able to fulfill all these roles if I don't get too caught up in any of them.

Stepping away from the stage, even for a moment, I'll see more clearly how the other actors in that particular scene are behaving and what is required of me. Sometimes, when we lose ourselves in a role, we allow others to put endless superficial demands upon us yet remain unable to satisfy those demands at a deeper level.

Soul-consciousness reduces the risk of that happening. As a mother, fully charged through my dedication, I won't need to reassure myself about my fitness for that role. I won't worry unduly about the whiteness of my laundry or the quality of my cakes. I will remain giving where it counts—of love, guidance, support, encouragement, joy. I'll give my children what they need without making demands in return, because I won't feel imposed upon. I don't cut myself off from my role, but by giving myself opportunities to recharge, I'll ensure that my perspective remains powerful and my motives positive.

THE HOUSE OCCUPIER

A spiritual metaphor with very down-to-earth, practical implications is that of the soul as the living inhabitant of a house or temple: the physical body. It's the awareness of the occupier, or dweller, and that which is occupied. Implicitly, we use this image when trying to catch someone's attention, tapping her on the shoulder and asking, Is anyone at home?

I am not my body, the place in which I dwell, but I am still responsible for its maintenance, well-being, and quality of atmosphere. After all, I spend a lot of time in it! When I keep it clean and fragrant and healthy, I can live in it comfortably.

There's plenty of rubbish waiting to enter. It can come in through the windows of my eyes and ears. Rubbish means the kind of information or stimulus that locks me into endless desires, forming negative reactions inside. Rubbish dirties my consciousness, taking me away from my positive truth.

My nose—stretching the metaphor further—is the front door: it is the first part of me that faces the world. If bitter winds blow and I don't know how to protect myself, I'll catch cold. Furthermore, if I am constantly looking for recognition and respect, my nose will soon be put out of joint.

In today's world, commercial and other interests constantly assault our senses. But if I am aware and alert, I will keep my house in order. If any rubbish gets in, I will soon clean it out again.

When I'm in a state of ignorance about myself, lost in the consciousness of the body, I tend to neglect or abuse the body. Through identifying with it, I am unable to care for it properly.

When my house is strong and clean and comfortable, it is easier for me to share positive qualities with others. My eyes show sweetness and contentment as I look upon the world.

My eyes also express whatever quality of wisdom I have. When I stay in the awareness that I am a soul, I see others in the same way, and instead of jealousy or competitiveness, there's a sense of the family of humanity.

Usually, on a physical level, I create all sorts of impressions of another person from just one glance—her age, gender, attractiveness, race, and nationality—and probably make various assumptions about her personality.

In the state of soul-consciousness, that changes. Looking out, I see souls, and I see them as my brothers. I see the sparkling star, the living being who dwells in that astonishingly complex home, the body, and an eternal bond between us is immediately apparent in which there can be honestly, acceptance, and friendship.

COMPONENTS OF THE SOUL

At Delphi, in Greece, there's a beautiful statue called *The Chari-oteer*. The figure depicted is not taking part in a race. From his steady gaze and regal appearance and the way he holds the reins, it's clear that he is representing the artist's vision of human potential, of a soul in full charge of the body. This is the classical counterpart of the image of the driver and car.

Being in charge of this body means I have to learn to discipline the physical senses. When they behave like wild horses, chasing off in different direction, my life becomes devoid of purpose and fulfillment. At times, it has seemed as if giving the senses free expression was liberating, but that was an illusion. Instead of being their master, I became subject to their whims and fancies.

Meditation enables me to take hold of the reins again. However, for this to work, I have to understand myself very well. Wrong ideas about the self have allowed my mind, as well as my senses, to become like a wild horse. In fact, for a long time the mind has been used to running with the senses, pulled by their physical attraction. Small wonder that when I finally decide I want peace of mind, I may have forgotten where to find it.

Therefore, I decide that I am going to look into who I am. Meditation means exploring my identity. The soul, the cognizant, living being, operates on different levels, and so my meditation will take me to different levels too.

When I create a space of silence and look within, the first layer of myself that I come to is that in which thoughts are bubbling into awareness. This is the mind. Understanding and accepting that this is a faculty of the soul, albeit it uses the brain for its expression, is a major step toward regaining control. The mind is one level of the energy of the soul. It's the level where I am creating thought. My thoughts and the feeling associated with them happen in my mind. They produce consequences that can be seen in the brain and elsewhere in the body, but their origin is in the mind.

When I look inward, I see that it is possible for me to guide the flow of these thoughts. Instead of allowing them to be jumbled and chaotic, I can direct them into a specific stream, concentrated, motivated, and purposeful. This is made possible by another dimension of my inner world: my capacity to understand and to choose between different possibilities. The word used in India for this capacity is *buddhi*. When functioning properly, it applies a quality control to my thoughts. *Buddhi* is sometimes translated as "intellect," and for the sake of simplicity, I'll use that word. It's not just a question of intellectual knowledge or cleverness, however, but of powerful awareness so that I can act on what I know.

The *buddhi* or intellect is like a vessel containing the power with which I can channel my thoughts and bring discipline to the energy of the mind. Knowledge is power, and as is the knowledge in my intellect, so will be my ability to select well from among the thoughts and feelings presented to me through the mind.

A well-developed intellect allows me to discriminate accurately between what is true and what is false. It serves as my conscience. It knows what is useful to me and what may cause me to lose my way.

At a deeper level than either mind or intellect lies a third faculty of the soul. This is a huge iceberg of information. It contains qualities original to me as a human soul, which I share with others, but in addition to that it includes a vast store of impressions that I carry as a result of my experiences in life and the individual way I have processed those experiences. These imprints help determine my unique personality and the way my mind functions.

Another useful word from the East, *sanskaras*, describes this fundamental level of my being. None of the English words that come closest to it—personality traits, imprints, impressions, unconscious—conveys sufficiently the depth of meaning of *sanskaras*, so I am going to borrow it here.

Think of the experiences I may have had in the course of an hour, the things I have heard, thought, felt, touched, tasted. Multiply that by the hours in a day—not just my waking hours but those I spend asleep too, when my mind is still functioning, processing the experiences of the day and putting them in a manageable format. All those data are recorded within my *sanskaras*. Multiply that by the days in a year and again by the years I have lived, and I begin to glimpse the magnitude of the information stored within my being.

They say that with an iceberg, nine-tenths of it is hidden below the waves. Often, the same is true of my *sanskaras*. I know only a fraction of my personality. This can be dangerous, as it may mean I can't trust my reactions to events. I don't know what I am going to say or do, especially in situations that I find stressful. Although I may be coping today, tomorrow I may go to pieces and behave in ways that shock me and others.

I'll reduce the risk of that happening if I take time to learn more about what lies below the surface. Notice that mind, intellect, and *sanskaras* are all idea-like: to do with the information, knowledge, and predispositions that contribute to my attitudes and behavior. Although they are energy in the sense that they are powerful, they are nonphysical and do not take up any space. They are functions of the tiny star that is the soul.

These divisions are somewhat artificial, since all three functions may be operating in simultaneous expression of the soul's energy. However, the model is extremely useful for informing my meditation and spiritual growth.

The model tells me that in response to events, my *sanskaras*, which are deep down, react in ways that give rise to thoughts, which are closer to the surface of my mind. Sometimes thoughts come into full, conscious awareness, but often they only reach the subconscious. In both cases, however, they may trigger actions that in turn either deepen existing *sanskaras* or give rise to new ones.

It is a cyclical process in which the soul develops its own unique package of responses to the situations life presents. Many of these ingrained responses are positive, but all of us also have negative habits of thought and behavior. Those habits cause pain to the self and to others around us (usually as a result of our trying to avoid further hurt to ourselves). Meditation allows me, perhaps for the first time in my life, to intervene deliberately, with understanding, in this process.

TAKING CONTROL

Meditation offers me powerful tools through which I can improve my character. This is because in meditation I am no longer just reacting to external stimuli but am looking at what is going on in the mind and consciously creating the types of thoughts I would like to have habitually.

I do this through the intellect. The intellect takes hold of the reins of the mind and chooses the direction in which to travel. When it does this repeatedly, my *sanskaras*—the imprints or tendencies within my character—start to change.

Soul-consciousness is the key to taking charge of what is going on in my mind. If I believe that my thoughts and feelings, including my sense of self, are simply consequences of brain processes, it means I've let go of the key. The more my consciousness is trapped in my physical identity, the more difficult it will be for me to discipline my mind.

In meditation, when I bring myself back to the knowledge that I am a soul and my intellect accepts and absorbs this awareness, I recognize that my thoughts are my own creation and that I can make choices about them. I realize that my natural state is to be the master of my mind, and I start taking charge of what is going on inside.

To illustrate the power of this process, let's take a situation where I am very much not in control: I have become angry, and my body is in a state of upheaval. My blood pressure is through the roof, my heart is racing, my digestive system is in a state of turbulence, and my cholesterol levels are up, along with all the stress hormones that mediate these reactions.

On top of that, I'm feeling the approach of a wave of remorse. I've done this enough times before to know the repercussions of my behavior. I've spoiled a relationship and worsened a situation. There is sorrow, guilt, and despair over my loss of control, a crisis of confidence in my self, and fear for my future. In that state of weakness, anger may come again. It's a vicious circle in which I trap myself—an addiction cycle. Addiction to a negative habit like anger is as bad as substance addiction.

A shaft of light can come shining through this darkness. That is when, in a moment, I remind myself that I am in fact a soul. Even while still caught up in the turmoil of my situation, I use my intellect to restore in myself, consciously and deliberately, as an act of will, the awareness of the point of light focused behind the eyes. In that moment, I am able to tap into the deep foundation of peace within my being. I calm

my mind by holding on to this awareness. I feel—I know—
that I *am* peace. As this experience grows, it penetrates my
whole physical system. Calm and stability are restored to my
body as well as my mind.

BUILDING STRENGTH

Meditation based on the model of the self as a spiritual being doesn't just help me clear things up after I have lost control. If I build the practice of soul-consciousness into my daily life, it also acts as preventive medicine and a tool for healing the soul itself, freeing it from harmful tendencies. It enables me to break through addictive cycles. In this way, it strengthens my physical health, too.

To begin with, when I'm experimenting with perhaps just a few minutes of meditation before launching into the day's work, my awareness of the true self soon slips once I'm engaged in action. I forget that I can be in charge of my thoughts and feelings. I'm liable to revert to my old pattern of reacting to events on an external level.

The more I practice and the deeper the experience is, the longer the effects last. Gradually, I become able to stay cool and clear in the busiest or most trying circumstances.

When you repeatedly underline something on a sheet of paper, the imprint deepens. Every time I give way to anger, the habit becomes stronger, and the aggression potentially more explosive.

Equally, every time I meditate and underline the awareness of the soul and the experience of peace and goodwill, the greater is the chance that this will be reflected in my behavior. My threshold of tolerance increases, where previously I had a short fuse, and as I become less reactive, I'm better able to face up to what needs to be said or done.

WHAT GOES WRONG?

We all exert some control over our thoughts, regardless of our philosophy. However, the more we lose ourselves in everyday action, the more our thoughts will tend to become reactions to what goes on outside us. Our lives will move in the same undirected way.

Then, when things don't work out as we might have wished, there is a human tendency either to blame other people and circumstances or to rationalize our pain by telling ourselves we are useless. Often, these two mental strategies go together. The trouble is that both are cop-outs, preventing us from going for a creative solution.

It's possible to lead life on a very superficial plane, without taking the time to sort out what is going on inside. Deeper difficulties are kept firmly locked away. I move from one diversion to another—eating, drinking, sleeping, enjoying the pleasures of the senses, changing my job, buying a new car or house, even having babies. All these are part of living, but if I make them my everything, it's as though they enable me to skate across the surface of life, and in time, an inner emptiness develops.

The feeling grows that "there must be more to life than

this." I find that my relationships are not working out as I would have hoped. I may perceive that they are lacking in depth. It begins to dawn on me that perhaps something is missing in the values I hold so that there has been a loss of integrity, and this has made me less dependable in my relationships than I could or should have been.

It's so easy to become caught up in my physical identity—my name and appearance, the family I was born into, the college I went to, the man or woman I married, the job I hold, the things I own. I forget my true identity, the spiritual being, and that it is me, the spirit or soul, who is experiencing life *through* this physical body and surrounding circumstances.

The physical, human side is essential, but the spirit—the being—makes the journey. It's through a spiritual consciousness that I'm able to access spiritual treasures of peace, of care, of love and joy. It is because we have so deprived ourselves of these treasures that there is an upsurge of interest in meditation.

The more I become trapped by a materialistic consciousness and the more I lose contact with my inner self, the less free I am to be myself. The pursuit of happiness through the physical senses brings very short-lived returns. My life lacks richness when the only things I know, understand, and feel are related to the information I receive from the physical senses, and I become divorced from the spiritual dimension.

The more I identify with the physical factors of my life, the more I become a hostage to fortune. If my self-respect is tied up with my physical appearance, how will I feel about myself when my beauty or my muscles have faded away or if I'm suddenly crippled and disfigured in a road accident? There's going to be an identity crisis.

The same will be true if my job is everything to me. If one day I have a good salary and position and the next day I am made redundant and nobody wants to know me, I will feel as if I have died. The distress is sometimes so great that people do, literally, lose their will to live.

It happens, too, in marriage, when someone loses a partner in whom they have invested all their own being. It also happens if my identity is tied to a bank balance or share holdings or business and suddenly I am broke.

All these are actually false perceptions, and the crazy part of living this way is that I can never be contented even while I succeed in maintaining my false identity. It's a case of either an inferiority complex or a superiority complex—both are unreal, and so both bring insecurity.

Even while I am externally successful, having my identity based on that success means I am enslaved. I've handed over my dignity. The unconscious knowledge of this enslavement will drive me into working even harder to keep up appearances. It's the addictive cycle at work again.

Meditation—looking at myself, seeing who I truly am, beginning to experience again the soul's intrinsic qualities of peace, love, and happiness—restores my ability to live in ways that are true to myself. I approach life from a much wider perspective. Meditation also enriches my relationships. Many blocks and barriers come between us when our perception and awareness are stuck in the physical dimension. If I know only 10 percent of myself and that is mostly on the surface, my relationships are going to be similarly superficial. When my self-respect is built on such shallow foundations, it will tend to be fragile and I'll be prone to trying to maintain it by dwelling on others' weaknesses, real or imagined. I'll also find it hard to acknowledge and appreciate their qualities. Such is the state of so many human relationships today.

In meditation, I go into the depths of myself, and there, within my inner being, I find a beauty and strength that automatically link me to the same qualities in others. I find qualities that are intrinsic to every soul: the original imprints or *sanskaras*. It's like a basic template for our humanity.

THE INNER TRUTH

ORIGINAL QUALITIES OF THE SOUL

Every human soul has *peace* as an original trait. It is fundamental to us. It's not a state of passivity but one of power. When, through my awareness of the soul, I separate myself from my body and surroundings, I immediately access that peace. There's a sense of a beauty and a harmony underlying existence.

Purity, in the sense of being completely clean, in a state of truth, is a second original quality of soul. This purity is also strength, like that of a flawless diamond. Where there are flaws, there is weakness and loss of value. Cracks develop, and there is discoloration.

Wisdom, a third quality innate to every one of us, is linked to both peace and purity. When my peace is disturbed, I am unable to hear the inner voice of wisdom. Flaws in my character distort the light of truth. When I forget that I have this wisdom available to me, I may go hunting for it in books and scripture and courses, but these things can never give me the complete picture. Wisdom is holistic and intuitive. It doesn't take me into unnecessary detail but shows me what I need to know at the right time.

A fourth fundamental quality within every human being is a state of *love*. Our experiences of life have sometimes been so traumatic that we cut ourselves off from the sweetness of this state of being, preferring to hide behind a hard exterior. But the reality is that in my original state, love is intrinsic to my nature.

Finally, there is *joy*. This is different from happiness, which we experience through the senses and which comes and goes according to circumstances. Joy doesn't require possessions. People who own nothing may experience it more than the wealthy. It is the joy of being alive—a joy so deep as to be like life itself, seeking to express itself whenever and wherever it can. However, worry, fear, and other negative thoughts and feelings block it.

In the East, teachings of ancient times describe the human body as being made of five elements, not in the way we know them in chemistry, but earth, air, water, fire, and ether. It was understood that balance was required among these five constituent properties, and ill health meant one or more was out of place.

It's useful to think of the soul as also consisting of five original constituent qualities and to recognize that when there is imbalance or deprivations in the experience of those qualities, the soul suffers. Many today find themselves in this condition.

Meditation enables me to feed myself with spiritual knowledge that gives me the experience of peace, purity, wisdom, love, and lasting happiness. It heals my wounds, removes the dirt, and nurtures the inner being. It gradually restores in me the confidence to emerge from the shadows— to live in the light of my original nature.

It is amazing, and heartwarming, when you rediscover these qualities beneath all the other impressions formed during a life that has probably been chaotic and unpleasant at times. There have been jealousies, possessiveness, greed, cynicism, desires, tantrums of the ego—all these have gone on in myself and others, leaving their mark on us all.

The journey of meditation bypasses negative tendencies and allows me to touch these original qualities, experience their truth, and express them in my life. It takes me back to the foundations of my being, of who I truly am and what I carry within me. I become more of a human being again, not just a human doing, and I relate to other people on that wider basis too.

The tools that Raja Yoga meditation provides for altering self-awareness are powerful and practical.

Because of the way they make use of the intellect, they can be implemented in everyday life. They challenge me, in fact, to make the effort to return repeatedly to the awareness that I am a spiritual being.

A Raja Yogi way of life requires me to be alert and present to immediate reality, not dreamy or disconnected. The goal is to bring the innate qualities of the soul into practical action and become a better person to be with—creative, productive, and fulfilled.

However, underpinning this process of change is the experience of another dimension of reality. This experience, which has been the goal of many traditional forms of meditation, is an altered state of consciousness. Within this state, deeper truths are perceived than are normally accessible, especially to adult, Western-educated minds.

The altered state is possible precisely because I am a spiritual being having a physical experience here on earth. Apart from my time here, playing my role on the stage, I also have an existence that is just of I, the soul, without this physical body. My ultimate home is offstage, in an unchanging, eternal dimension where there is just light and stillness. It lies beyond the material world of constant movement and change.

There's a moment when any actor can take off his costume and go home—there is no role remaining, no more performance, just a period of rest. Meditation helps me come to that experience of stepping away from the stage and from my responsibilities and come back to the pure consciousness that is at the core of my being.

As in the near-death experience, well documented in recent years, there can be a feeling of the soul as a being of light, traveling in a state of bliss to a space of infinite light, in a place of silence, beyond all fluctuation.

An actor doesn't remain offstage constantly. In the same way, it would be unnatural and unrealistic for me to try to remain constantly in this silent home of the soul. But being aware of it reassures me that my spirituality is firmly rooted in reality. It is also valuable to experience the consciousness of this other dimension from time to time, because even a moment's experience of it brings enormous rest and refreshment to both soul and body.

With my battery recharged, an inner strength carries me

through all the things I need to do. Here is an exercise in Touching the Light:

Sitting quietly, letting my body be comfortable, but not so relaxed that I fall asleep, I focus my thoughts in the awareness of I, the soul, as an infinitesimal point with infinite energy . . . I come to the consciousness of being a shining star, a being of light . . . With the power of my thought, I step away from this physical costume . . . I see my physical body sitting quietly in this room . . . for a few moments, I move beyond the world of matter into the dimension of light . . . I, the being of light, surrounded by infinite light . . . I am in a place where there are no walls, only light . . . no movement, no sound, only stillness . . . I feel very comfortable here . . . I have a sense of belonging, a feeling that this is my home . . . I feel full, content . . . I am aware, conscious, yet silent and still in this place of unbroken purity . . . a purity that is constant, eternal . . . and my own stage of purity emerges and resonates with the purity of my surroundings . . . I am pure, I am peaceful, I am full . . . and from here, I look down on the planet below . . . I see the activity, the movement, the attraction . . . but for a few moments more,

I stay in a state of rest, in my home . . . And now with the power of my thoughts, I move away from that land of silence and come back onto the stage of the world, into this room, into the awareness of my physical costume . . . And as I return, I keep the experience of sweet silence with myself to use as a resource while I play my role on the stage of the world.

THE NATURE OF ETERNITY

From the moment the soul has occupied the physical body, it has been living a life increasingly dominated by limits. These are not just physical limits of strength or size, income or possessions, but of time—the time a relationship lasts, the time it takes me to perform a task, the time I spend asleep.

In meditation, when I step out of the consciousness of the body and touch the pure consciousness of the soul, I'm stepping out of both space and time. I begin to get a feel for my own eternity, in which I simply am without beginning or end. I exist after it has returned to dust.

This awareness of the eternity of my identity is powerful because it removes the fear of death. With that goes a lot of the ego-driven, compulsive behavior, the desperate need to make a mark through my work or possessions or offspring, which comes when there isn't the realization of my immortality.

I, the soul, become aware of a continuity to my existence. I become able to have the feeling of a place that is my eternal home, a place of silence, of rest, of peace. It is my place of origin, but not in the sense that something comes out of nothing. I exist in that home, and I come from that home to play my role, and I return there when my role is completed. Even as this realization returns, I can feel fear falling away and my heart becoming full.

BACK TO NORMAL

Meditation is neither a flight of fancy nor an intellectual indulgence. It is a necessity for me to be able to function in a proper way, as a normal human being, in the real world, right now.

A heart full of peace, love, and joy is a healthy heart, and health means normality. Yet we have become so deviant from our truly normal states that we do not realize what has happened to us. We think it is normal to be fearful, angry, and peaceless, at least sometimes. Or we feel that it is normal to use drink and drugs, or the television set, or any of a multiplicity of other addictions to numb our chronically stressed feelings.

There's said to be a frog that adjusts so well to changes in temperature that it won't jump out of a pot even when the water is nearly boiling. So it dies! Meditation lets me jump out of the pot. It means understanding how I turn up the heat in my own life and how I can turn it down again, how I create thought and feeling, and how I can draw on my original qualities to better my experience of life.

THOUGHTS AND FEELINGS

The uppermost area of the mind, very familiar to us, is the area of conscious thought. Thoughts surface into awareness like bubbles. Many thoughts carry with them a feeling or feelings, and again, we are all familiar with that. The thought "I like the look of that cream cake," for example, could be accompanied by feelings of hunger, or greed, or joy, or longing, or anticipated satisfaction.

Less commonly understood is the insight offered by Raja Yoga, supported by my own experience in the spiritual domain, that feelings, as well as thoughts, originate within the soul.

Feelings are clearly reflected in physical changes in the body: I may feel my heart race with excitement, my mouth salivate with anticipation, and my stomach sink with fear. This is because soul and body function in complementary ways, so that what goes on in the soul is definitely reflected in the body and vice versa. It's not that feelings arise out of the blue or solely as a reaction to external stimuli. They come from me, the soul. Recognizing this is an invaluable step toward breaking free from cycles of unwanted or inappropriate thoughts and feelings.

However, when I create thoughts that have a feeling component, those feelings have an impact on the soul as well as the body. The longer I experience thoughts and feelings of a particular variety, the greater is the soul's predisposition to generate those feelings. This can reach the point where feelings take over and I experience their impact even though I no longer consciously connect them with my thoughts.

Let's say, for example, my partner has done something without consulting me, and there's a pattern of thoughts running through my mind, such as "Why are they doing this? It shouldn't have happened like this. How dare they! Why on earth didn't they ask me? I do wish they wouldn't be so stupid. It would have been much better if it was done like that," and so on. Turning over thoughts of this type in my mind leaves me with a feeling that is definitely not positive—it's critical, rejecting, hard done by.

What is worse, when I have let feelings like this emerge, it is all too easy to carry them over into circumstances where they have no relevance. I have left home for work, perhaps, and in my thoughts I am now dealing with completely different issues, but the unpleasant critical feelings are still with me to the point where they affect my behavior. I react over some minor provocation, creating bad feeling in others as well. Or perhaps it works the other way around, and I carry bad feelings from a rotten day at work back into the home and then rationalize my feelings by creating an atmosphere of antagonism where there should be comfort and support and love.

Over a period, we can build up an enormous tangle of thought and feeling in this way, creating many unnecessary difficulties. Meditation helps me untangle this mess and come to grips with what is going on in my own inner world. It helps me understand how I create thoughts and feelings, how to take responsibility for them, and how to tap into my original, positive qualities and displace negative patterns. Thus, meditation is far from being a luxury.

To get the positive cycle working in my life, the easiest place to start with is thought. It's easy to change thought. It just requires attention. And through changing thought, it's easy to change feelings. I decide that for a few minutes, or even a few moments, I am going to set aside negative thoughts, which are weak or wasteful, and create pure, positive, powerful thoughts, based on awareness of my spiritual identity. I remember that I am a soul, a being of inherent peace, purity, love, joy, and wisdom, nonphysical and eternal. As I do this, I begin to experience those original qualities of the self. Positive and empowering feelings emerge.

If I keep in contact with myself to check what my feelings are like and maintain the meditative awareness whenever I have the chance, I will find that the good feelings I have experienced through conscious choice carry over into my dealings with others. Then, in any exchange, although the other person's words or actions may not be to my liking, I'll be better able to maintain a good feeling toward that individual and toward myself.

For example, I leave home and find myself in a situation at a bus stop where two people are arguing. One of them perhaps gets aggressive with me as well, but the feelings of peace I experienced in my meditation are still with me, and so I don't add fuel to the flames by reacting angrily or fearfully. In fact, if my peace is powerful enough, it will cool the others down.

To become a donor of positive feelings in this way is a priceless achievement. It is good for my own well-being and for contributing to the creation of a harmonious atmosphere wherever I am.

EMOTIONS AND SANSKARAS

The deeper I take my exploration of the soul, the greater the power that becomes available to me: the power to know myself, respect myself, be true to myself, and help others access their own truth, too.

Beneath the level of thoughts and feelings lie emotions and *sanskaras*. *Sanskaras* are the imprints left on the soul by experience, arising from its actions and relationships, and emotions are very close to these imprints: they are impulses associated with the *sanskaras*.

Thus, the simplest, cyclical description of the soul's functioning, where thought gives rise to action, action gives rise to *sanskaras*, and *sanskaras* give rise to further thoughts, now has two additional components.

Next up from *sanskaras* are the emotions; then come feelings and then thoughts. Emotions are deeper than either thoughts, which I can catch instantly, or feelings, which I will be able to see if I stop and check. Emotions are very close to the *sanskaras*, and just as we can't see all the *sanskaras* of an individual, we can't always see that individual's emotions.

Feelings, being more toward the surface, are more clearly identified, but you have to go deeper to see the quality of emotions and the quality of *sanskaras*. As with feelings, when emotions are stirred, this is reflected in physiological changes—chemical and electrical activity in the body. It's the same with anything that the soul experiences. Pain, hunger, heat and cold, pleasure, satisfaction, and comfort are all mediated by the body, though it is the soul that perceives and experiences these conditions.

However, strong emotions don't affect just the body; they also have an impact on the soul. Understanding this is vital to understanding ourselves and learning how to change.

When the soul suffers emotional trauma from which there is lasting impact, brain and body will reflect the continuing strain. Brain chemical production is likely to be affected, and there may also be permanent feelings of tiredness. But the trauma at the root of these physical effects is at that deep level within the soul itself, and the resulting emotional sensitivity will also stem from the soul.

If, for example, I suffer a series of blows that cause me to become lacking in self-respect, there will be a *sanskara* to that effect, and I'll show a tendency to react with tears or anger whenever there is a setback that touches this sensibility. A person who does not have this tendency will be much less readily provoked.

Thoughts may be transient. Feelings, which accompany repeated thought patterns, stay a bit longer. But when the soul suffers a loss that it is not able to deal with, it becomes emotionally damaged and the consequences can be extreme.

If feelings that come to me because of bereavement, for example, can be catered to and cared for at that time through prayer, meditation, or family support, I will deal with the feelings and move on.

If, however, I am unable to draw on such support, whether from God or from human beings, the sense of loss I feel is going to cause deeper damage. Then it will not just be a feeling of loss, but it will actually have wounded the soul. Until that wound heals, I'll carry it with me long after the loss has been suffered. The emotions linked to it will surface repeatedly, though I may have no idea where my sorrow is coming from. I'll be unable to stay happy no matter how favorable my circumstances may be today.

Meditation does not require or encourage me to go delving into the subconscious or unconscious roots of my pain. Instead, through thought, it enables me to take conscious control of my feelings and emotions so as to displace the negative, which brings sorrow, with the positive, which brings happiness.

Just as my thoughts and feelings can be negative or positive, the same is true of my emotions and *sanskaras*. When we describe somebody today as being emotional, that tends to be pejorative because many of the *sanskaras* and associated emotional tendencies that catch our attention are negative.

However, emotions can also be pure, healthy, and strong. The passion, as well as compassion, that Mother Teresa brought to her work for the poor gave her the drive with which to serve both tirelessly and effectively. Raja Yoga meditation enables the soul to experience pure, powerful emotions and loving feelings to such an extent that the wounds left by past experiences are healed. Raja Yoga means "royal union"—it means embarking on a love affair with God.

The experience of God's love is a healing balm for my emotions and a remedy for the pain the soul feels. Before we can fully understand and take benefit from that relationship, however, we must complete our exploration of our own consciousness. What caused us to forget our divinity so that we became lost and wounded souls? What is now required of me if I am to recover and maintain my consciousness of the truth, my awareness of myself as a soul?

MAINTAINING SOUL-CONSCIOUSNESS

Sitting quietly in meditation, using my intellect to remind me that I am a soul, and experiencing the beauty of the state in which the soul is aware of itself as truly distinct from the body is the essence of the task I have before me. Simply by giving time to practice this awareness, I will move forward.

Connected with this is the importance of maintaining soul-consciousness through the day as I engage in activity. This is less straightforward, because there is a strong, deeply ingrained habit pulling us away from the consciousness of the soul, back into body-consciousness. Soul-consciousness is like quicksilver: one moment it is there, the next it is gone.

Images that reinforce my spiritual sense of identity, such as those of the actor on the stage and the driver of the car, are valuable tools for the intellect as it undertakes the job of helping to change the way I think, feel, and act. However, the bottom line for self-change is to change the nature of my actions.

When I recognize myself as a soul and draw on the original and eternal qualities of the soul for my sense of identity, I feel fulfilled. The qualities are there, deep in my being. I don't have to go looking for them outside myself. And being spiritual, they are unlimited. It is like drawing from a bottomless well. I can drink to my heart's content.

However, I must also open my heart and pass on to others the strength I have received. Otherwise, my spirituality becomes a dead end. The bucket with which I draw from the well can't be refilled unless I am also prepared to keep emptying it. That doesn't mean I have to make myself spiritually drained, just that the more I give—with my actions always coming from a positive perspective—the more I am able to receive.

Therefore, I consciously let go of the negative habits of thought, feeling, and behavior that accompanied my previous body-conscious condition. I stop criticizing others, demanding respect from others, or being fearful of others—habits all resulting from seeking to define myself in comparison to others. I let go of jealousy, greed for wealth or position, and possessiveness toward those close to me. I root out egoism, which prevents me from acknowledging my mistakes, and anger, which obliterates both peace and truth within the soul, blinding me to the needs and feelings of others. I also drop habits of cynicism, depression, and low self-esteem that may have developed when the soul was in its depleted state.

I see very clearly that all these behaviors were linked to my previous condition of ignorance about myself and that now that I am developing soul-consciousness, they no longer serve any purpose. In fact, they are obstacles to the growth of my spiritual awareness. No matter how much I try, I won't be able to continue to meditate unless I bring the positive feelings available to me in meditation into my actions as well. The intellect will not be able to maintain the effort of disciplining the mind and changing the *sanskaras*.

POSITIVE AND NEGATIVE

Much is spoken these days about positive and negative thoughts and behavior, but the distinction is not always clear. It seems at times that when people tell me to be positive, they just want me to support their plan or opinion. I may not see anything to be so positive about in what they are doing!

A useful question to use as criterion for evaluating true positivity is, "Does this thought, word, or action lead me toward the truth of the original state of being of the soul, or is it taking me farther away from that?" When, through meditation, I have come back to the realization that the underlying truth about all souls is a state of peace, love, purity, joy, and natural wisdom, I have a touchstone with which to check. Am I bringing others and myself closer to those original qualities? At the spiritual level, there is a connectedness between us that ensures that if I help others in this regard, I will also help myself, whereas if I harm others, that will also harm me.

We live in times when we don't like to use the word "sin." One reason is the judgmental overtones. Contrary to the biblical injunction to "let him that is without sin among you cast the first stone," religious-minded people in particular have sometimes been all too ready to condemn others. Another reason, however, has to do with what has been going on inside our own awareness. There is a time when our consciousness—and with that, the conscience—is so clean and clear that whatever is right and true is naturally followed and nothing else filters through into our words and actions.

A secondary state is when my conscience acknowledges that which is the truth but does not have the strength to be able to enact the truth. The conscience tells me one thing, but my feelings pull me elsewhere, and my feelings get the better of me. I do what I know I shouldn't.

When this happens repeatedly, the conscience weakens further, until its voice is silenced. I can no longer discriminate between truth and falsehood. I feel that there is no right and wrong, that everything is relative, that each one's standards are his or her own.

The experience of the original qualities of the self in meditation and the understanding in Raja Yoga that these qualities are common to all souls show me that absolute standards of right and wrong, positive and negative, do exist. "Positive" takes in all the aspects that put me in touch with and enhance my original qualities, through my own experience of them and through their expression in interaction with others. "Negative" does the reverse. It hides my truth and causes me to stumble around, ignorantly, hurting myself and others yet not knowing how or why.

All of us are affected by this positive/negative fluctuation. It affects our thoughts, feelings, and emotions, but most of all, deep down, we carry these contrasting predispositions in our *sanskaras*, which form our character. The goal of my meditation is to shape a new character for myself, strengthening positive *sanskaras* and eroding the negative tendencies.

TRANSFORMATION

If you've ever tried to give up smoking, you know the will-power it takes to change even a single habit. Yet I've seen amazingly rapid transformations in human behavior through the practice of meditation. That is because there is one simple method through which all positive attributes are restored. It was through forgetting that one method that we lapsed into the negative.

No matter how much negativity I may have been attacked by, no matter how much I carry that negativity even within my *sanskaras*, awareness of the soul can bring instant change. It's like suddenly glimpsing an Old Master underneath inferior work when a painting is being restored. A turning point has occurred.

However, full restoration takes time. The excitement of the discovery allows the rest of the cleaning work to happen automatically, joyously. That is what accurate meditation can do for me.

In the awareness of the soul, my own original qualities are immediately accessible to me. When I forget my eternal identity as the point of light, I find myself drawn back again into the identity of the body, with all its needs and desires. My negative *sanskaras* developed through that false identification, and they express themselves when I return to that limited consciousness. Equally, they lose their hold on me as soon as I practice soul-consciousness again.

In soul-consciousness, I am free and generous-hearted with others. In body-consciousness, my self-respect depends on my position in society, my possessions and appearance, and people I like to call my own. I will try to have a hold over them, to bind them to me. Yet the reality is that I don't even know how long I will have the privilege of using this body. There are certainly no guarantees for my relationships and possessions. The more I try to bind them to me, the more I will suffer.

The deeper my body-consciousness, the more possessive and dependent I become. I'll want to hang on to everything—status, wealth, people, money, the past, my opinions. In fact, at its worst I become like a fossil. Nothing flows through me anymore except a lot of fear because of my limited consciousness. Love becomes very scarce. It's remarkable that the consequences of such a tiny slip of misidentification are so enormous.

This is the fall, symbolized in the story of Adam and Eve. The forbidden fruit from the Tree of Knowledge, which caused banishment from the Garden of Eden, wasn't knowledge in the sense of truth, which is liberating, but the consciousness of the body. We replay this story ourselves, losing all our treasures of lasting happiness, by overidentifying with the body and losing sight of the soul.

Every aspect of negativity starts with this misconception about who I am. When I lose sight of myself as a soul, I am no longer the ruler of my senses: they pull me from my state of truth. I lose my strength, my self-sovereignty, and my self-respect.

In soul-consciousness, I regain my reality and sovereignty. I know I am the one in charge of this physical body, and I use the body to express my feelings, to share my thoughts, to get into action, and to receive information from the world around me. This is the right way to use my senses.

POWER AND RESPONSIBILITY

Developing the consciousness of myself as a soul is simple, but I need to nurture this awareness with a sense of responsibility. When I begin my day with meditation, it means I am reinforcing the positive thoughts, feelings, and *sanskaras* within me. Then, when I come into action and relationship with others, these positive attributes will influence my attitude and vision toward them and my behavior.

In this way, as I change, the world around me changes, because the energy I am bringing into my circumstances is positive. As my own little world changes, it touches the lives of others, and the ripples spread.

In body-consciousness, when the repercussions of my negativity catch up with me, my heart shrinks and so does my world. I tend to cut myself off from other people or find some comfort zone that restricts my interactions. In soul-consciousness, I realize that my potential is enormous. I can make a difference to a thousand—or a hundred thousand—just by accepting responsibility for the self.

I recognize that I am responsible for the choices I make in my life. I am responsible for my thoughts, feelings, and emotions and the way my personality turns out. I am responsible for my responses to people and circumstances. If, previously, I lost the ability to respond in the right way, I now know how to restore it.

Meditation teaches me how to create thoughts that are good and true and feelings that will bring lasting happiness for me and others. It shows me how to handle myself in life in a way that removes inner emptiness and the fear, hostility, and addictive behaviors that went with it. This in itself gives me the strength to respond positively.

"Addiction"—which means literally "without a say"— arose when I didn't have that strength. Substance addiction is familiar to us, but it is less widely recognized that personality traits such as ego, anger, and greed are also addictions, as is attachment or possessiveness. All arise in an attempt to fill the emptiness we feel; all represent a grasping after short-lived satisfaction, but ultimately this comes only at the expense of other people, the environment, and ourselves. No matter how much is taken in this way, there is always a need for more.

In our consumerist, materialistic society, expression of sensual desires and their satisfaction have been encouraged and have seemed like fun. This is especially true in the area of physical relationships. In wanting to make another person my own, however, I become a slave to my own passion. Or the sex drive becomes separated from its role in relationships, and its constant stimulation is made into a commodity and a lucrative means to sell other goods and services.

An important part of liberation is the desire to achieve it. As long as I think lust, ego, possessiveness toward others, greed, and anger are just part of life, I'll accept them in myself as well. If that's my choice, then perhaps, for me, the addictions are mild and I haven't yet been disappointed by them or seen how dangerous they can be.

For many in today's world, however, as we witness a rise in violence in society, the buildup of anger, the damage caused by ego, the breakdown in relationships, the greed and corruption and loss of a sense of social responsibility, there's an awakening going on. An inner voice says that there must be a better way.

Coming back to the awareness of the soul, I know what that way is. When I experience the power of peace and natural fullness of my being in meditation, the need to indulge in addictive escapist behaviors as a means of trying to fill the void in my heart becomes less. I recover the strength to take responsibility again for my thoughts, feelings, and actions.

In soul-consciousness, my conscience regains the power

to guide me beyond the pull of the mind so that I am attentive to the quality of my actions. I recognize how my addictions arose and how they destroyed my inner freedom and independence. Their hold on me lessens, and my habits of thought and feeling become more positive. I learn to move beyond the influence of the senses and of negative emotions.

I stop selfishly trying to change other people as a means of avoiding the need to face up to changing myself. I recognize that peace of mind, born of truth and divinity, is my most priceless asset. I resolve to restore it in myself as the best healing gift I can offer to a troubled world.

BREAKING FREE

Soul-consciousness is a discipline that sets me free. When I practice and experience the awareness of myself as a soul in meditation, my positive attributes become accessible, and I move toward expressing my full potential. I learn how to escape the vicious circle in which body-conscious thoughts, feelings, actions, and *sanskaras* were pulling me down through a kind of spiritual entropy. I recover value for myself.

The goal is to regain such a natural awareness of the soul that it stays with me through the whole day, in everything I do. I have found three methods helpful in developing this consciousness:

1. Taking just a few seconds, every hour, to jot down in a notebook the extent to which I have been able to maintain the awareness of myself as a soul. If the answer is zero, that's okay: it stimulates attention for the next period.

2. Every few hours, to stop whatever I am doing for two or three minutes and turn my attention within, creating the awareness and feeling of the

soul. At Raja Yoga centers around the world, where music plays at fixed times to mark this break, we call it traffic control. It slows the traffic of our thoughts, reducing the risk of accidents.

3. Every time I sustain the body with food or drink, I pause for a moment to sustain the soul as well with thoughts of the divine, the nonphysical dimension of being, and the peace and love associated with it.

EYES-OPEN MEDITATION

Soul-consciousness, my experience in meditation, and the quality of my character and life are deeply connected with another factor, which seems at first to be very physical but which is integral to my progress: the practice of meditating with my eyes open. There are several reasons for this.

The most important is that my aim is to bring a spiritual awareness into my whole life, not just keep meditation as a private enjoyment. It's true that the positivity and peace associated with meditation will in any case carry over into my actions, but this influence will last longer if I have learned eyes-open meditation.

In turn, that improves the chances that when I next sit to meditate, it will be easy to return to an awareness of the divine. Eyes-open meditation enables me to practice seeing other people with soul-conscious vision. This practice is formalized when people learning Raja Yoga meditate in a group. An experienced yogi sits at the front of the group and lets his or her gaze rest at the center of the forehead of each of the other meditators in turn, with the awareness that behind the eyes is the spark of cognizant energy, the eternal being that we call the soul. Others in the group do the same so that when our eyes meet, we are connecting our thoughts in remembrance of the divine.

When I leave the meditation and meet other people, that practice continues. I may be speaking or listening to somebody, but I'll have the awareness that that person is a soul. This gives me a sense of an eternal bond between us and allows communication to take place without fear, at a deeper level than usual. I'll connect not just through sight or sound or touch but with pure love. There won't be any other feeling or emotions in the way.

Otherwise, human reactions are such that we see other people's gender, or the color of their skin, or their age, and perhaps a host of other physical features, and our relationships are distorted by these superficial observations. As William Blake, the English poet, put it:

> *This life's five windows of the soul*
> *Distorts the Heavens from pole to pole,*
> *And leads you to believe a lie*
> *When you see with, not thro', the eye.*

Meditating with the eyes open enables me to practice seeing through the eye. It teaches me to remain in the awareness that it is I, the soul, who is seeing, I, the soul, who is experiencing the world through all five senses. This consciousness defeats the overidentification with the body that so distorts my attitude and vision. It allows me to stay in the awareness of the spiritual dimension while remaining connected to the world around me.

This is an enormously useful knack that makes it possible to live life with both love and detachment. The lotus flower, an ancient symbol of spirituality, illustrates this goal: its stem connects it to the mud at the bottom of the pond, but its petals stay above, facing the sky.

2 | GOD

AN INHERITANCE OF TRUTH

Meditation works wonders as a technique to aid relaxation or teach concentration. For me, however, it has become much more than that. It is a means to communicate with God and to receive from God a power of truth that enables me to live in ways that are true to myself. The more I have benefited in this way, the more I have learned to love and understand God.

The power received from God in meditation enables me to transform myself spiritually so that I feel myself to be accumulating a great fortune. The way I think, feel, and act today determines what happens to me tomorrow, and through connecting with God in meditation, my thoughts, feelings, and actions become more consistently positive. As narrow self-concerns fall away, the giving aspect of my nature, original to all of us but obscured by body-consciousness, comes to the fore.

Previously, the soul was progressively losing its truth. With meditation, that trend is reversed. Consequently, I feel my future is more secure. I have rediscovered my truth and the One who can help me make that truth my own again.

It is like coming into an inheritance after reestablishing

contact with a loving but long-forgotten parent. Since the inheritance is a spiritual one rather than part of the physical world, it cannot be taxed, stolen, or otherwise compromised by anyone other than myself. The happiness that comes with the awareness of such a fortune is deep and lasting.

OPENING THE HEART

Meditation means allowing the mind to dwell on aspects of eternal truth. One part of that is the awareness of the eternal identity of the soul. The second is awareness of God as a supreme and unchanging source of truth.

It's a joy to me that we are not as shy of using God's name as we were even a few years ago (though I have difficulty today with "His" as a pronoun—while used here for simplicity, "He" and "His" are not meant to imply a male form).

Certainly, thirty years ago in England, when people said they would like to learn about yoga, they would often add that they did not want to hear anything about God. The climate has changed. I feel we are ready to discover more about this being who is called God.

Perhaps that is because there has been the opportunity to explore other concepts and philosophies in which God did not feature and we have found them wanting. Perhaps also, seeing the problems the world faces, we have realized that we cannot do the job of making a better world on our own.

I used to be reluctant to touch on the topic of God. Growing up in my teens in London, I was exposed to Hinduism through my family and to a certain amount of Christianity through

school, and I had many Jewish friends. The difficulty for me had
been to get answers on the subject of God that would touch both
my head and my heart.

I felt that the concept present in much Eastern philosophy, of
God as an all-pervading energy, had an appealing universality.
Yet what was the nature of that nature, such that it could help
me personally? I also found it hard to understand how there
could be a being who was supreme—the Highest-on-High—
yet with whom one could have a personal relationship.

On the other hand, when people spoke of finding fulfillment or salvation by relating to God in human form, that
did not seem as if it could be the whole story. My heart could
recognize the love and faith this helped inspire, but my head
was not satisfied. The image of Krishna as God's true incar-
nation, for example, was not appealing for most people in the
West, and the image of Christ as the being who is God did
not appeal to most in the East.

East or West, I felt distaste for the exclusivity and divisive-
ness that religion seemed capable of engendering, although
it was clear to me that this was a product of human interpretation rather than divine will.

The beauty of meditation is that it can bring us to a
shared, universal understanding of God, no matter what our

religious or philosophical background, by taking us into the experience of God as a being of light. Whatever our distinctive faith or philosophy, it will be enhanced by this spiritual experience.

ENTERING THE SPIRITUAL DOMAIN

To open my heart to God, I need first to bring into focus the understanding of myself as a being of light, nonphysical and eternal. This direct experience of my own deepest reality frees my mental energies from the pull of matter and gives rise to thoughts and feelings of love for the divine. It's like cleaning the metal contact plate in an electrical switch so that the current will flow smoothly again. I have to free my mind of the tarnish of body-consciousness.

I remind myself that I, the self or soul, am an infinite point of light, dimensionless in terms of the physical world. My true home is a domain of peace, beyond the flux of worldly events, outside time.

There, I exist as a tiny star, like a seed, containing within me the potential for everything that I am to be and do on the stage of the world when the time comes for me to play my part. My skills, my talents, my strengths and weaknesses, my aspirations, my dreams, everything I ever experience—the blueprint for all this is within the soul. It's a huge resource that I can access when I come back to the awareness of the eternal nature of the soul.

In this consciousness of I, the soul, as a living light,

nonphysical and eternal, it becomes possible for me to approach the subject of God. It is actually quite simple. Mystics of all religions have spoken of God as light. The question that arises is, What kind of light?

It's a light that seems to have life, that radiates love, that gives a sense of knowing and belonging, a light that is able to give comfort and remove fear. It isn't physical light, yet it is illumination. It's described as the light of pure consciousness—of love, of truth, of wisdom, of bliss.

The beauty and simplicity of God, in the understanding and experience offered by Raja Yoga, is that He has positive attributes that are the same as the innate qualities of all human beings, but to an infinite degree—just a point of light, infinite, like all souls, but ever full, with nothing to detract from the original qualities, which are therefore limitless.

Every human soul possesses these qualities, but to different degrees. This is a fact of nature, arising from the fact that we have different parts to play in the world. We also differ in the extent to which we lose sight of those original qualities in the course of playing our parts.

Because of His unchanging qualities, however, God is able to serve as a reference point for that which is highest in humans. This is the wonderful secret for drawing on God's power: to understand that my original nature is also God's nature and that it is my right, as a child of the Supreme, to replenish my truth in relationship with this spiritual parent. All God asks of me is that I should keep bringing my mind back to Him and stop performing the selfish, body-conscious actions that obscure the relationship.

B. K.
JAYANTI

76

MAKING THE CONNECTION

In meditation, I move my consciousness away from the body and into the awareness of the soul so that my mind can go beyond the distractions of the physical world and into the realm of infinite light that is the spiritual dimension. There, I focus my mind on God as a point of light and allow myself to connect with the qualities of the Supreme.

I encounter a mind that is an ocean of peace and of love. There is also an intelligence, holding all wisdom, with an infinite capacity for understanding, and a complete benevolence, never demanding, only bestowing.

Let's experiment with this. It's useful first to designate a specific place in your home as your meditation corner or room so that it develops the right associations. As far as possible, it should be quiet and comfortable and without distractions.

Sitting up straight, gazing ahead, but with your attention turned inward, try the following thoughts. You may read them at first, but then just gently lead your mind in a similar direction:

> *I take a few long, deep breaths . . . As I observe myself*
> *doing so, I can feel my thoughts slowing down . . . Within*

my mind, I create the image of my eternal identity . . . the spark of light, the life in this physical costume . . . I detach my consciousness from its identification with matter and come to the awareness of the eternal being . . . With the power of my mind, I, the soul, move into a realm of light, beyond all physical pulls . . . In this place of light I come to the Supreme . . . I see the Supreme as a point of light, an infinite spark . . . From the Supreme, I begin to feel waves of peace and love reaching me . . . After such a long time, it's so refreshing . . . I'm connecting again with the Supreme . . . and as waves of peace surround me, I absorb peace within my being . . . radiate peace into the world.

Keeping the connection with the ocean of peace, I carry peace with me as I return to the awareness of my physical surroundings. I can practice, in turn, connecting with God as the ocean of peace, of love, of wisdom, of purity, and of bliss. God's attributes are said to be as vast as the ocean, but these five qualities contain the essence. And when the soul fills with these qualities in meditation, it is able to experience its own highest nature.

In the physical world, opposites attract; in the spiritual domain, like connects with like. This is why the first step in meditation is to practice soul-consciousness, through which I'm able to discipline my mind and create a degree of peace within myself. Then I'll be able to connect with God quickly, when I wish, and receive the experience of those unlimited qualities.

Thus, soul-consciousness not only allows me to begin to understand God, it tunes my mind to the right frequency for experiencing God and the qualities of the divine.

If, through the day, my mind has been caught in the flux of people and events and has become restless, peaceless, and probably unfeeling as well, I'll have driven myself far from God and the connection will be harder to make. When I live as part of the rat race, becoming mechanical and subhuman in the quality of my thoughts and actions, small wonder that the Source of the highest qualities seems distant. However, bringing myself back to the consciousness of the soul, I'm always able to move in the direction where I can start knowing God.

The connection I make with God is my personal, subjective experience. I can listen to lectures about God, I can read about God, I can hear many beautiful things about God, but only through my own practice of soul-consciousness and by experimenting with this idea of focusing my mind on the Supreme can I come to an experience of God and receive the benefit accordingly.

The experience is subjective, but that does not mean God is not a reality. Even in a human relationship, it's my own thoughts and perceptions that connect me with people. The words I share with them and the actions I engage in with them come later, but first it's a connection of minds. The closer the connection of minds is, the deeper and more rewarding will be the exchange within the relationship.

The same is true of my relationship with God. In my mind, I envisage the Supreme as a point of light, a seed of vast potential like myself, although in God's case the ultimate Seed, with the highest attributes. Through this mental connection, I attune to the qualities inherent in the Supreme.

DEEPENING THE RELATIONSHIP

As I get to know God, the relationship deepens. I realize that although He is seedlike, a point of reference, God also has personality—of truth, of beauty, of benevolence, of giving. How is this possible?

We normally think of a seed as inert despite its enormous potential. But when I link my mind to God's, its clear to me that He is anything but inert. The energy within God is subtle in that it is nonphysical, but it is also radiant like light, and in meditation I can catch that radiance, absorb it, and feel its warmth and wisdom healing me and making me whole.

I can also see God's greatness at work in others. When I see virtue around me, I know that ultimately this comes from God. I'm aware, too, that some people stay so true to God in how they live that they enable others to experience the radiance of the divine. Prophets, saints, mystics, and the founders of the great religions have also contributed to our feeling for God through their lives and teachings.

Despite these examples, however, violence, selfishness, and suffering do not seem to have diminished and have probably increased if we look behind the facade of material prosperity. The need of our times is for something more direct. My experience is that the Supreme Soul, recognizing this need, is shining the light of His pure thought more brightly than ever into the world, inviting us to reclaim for ourselves the inheritance of truth by drawing on the qualities inherent in the Supreme and making them our own.

MOTHER AND FATHER

The relationship can develop at many levels. For example, particularly at the beginning and end of the day, there is special value in relating to God as my spiritual parent. Giving time to sweet inner conversation and loving experience with my Supreme Father and Mother, I become equipped with the emotional resources needed to stay strong in the face of life's challenges.

Physical parents do their best, but at the human level, the impressions left on our minds by childhood years are often mixed. Therefore, I leave aside all those memories, good and bad, and in soul-consciousness I find I can draw on such an unlimited source of goodness as to make God the perfect parent.

As the Supreme Father, God is like the sun, radiating the energy of truth, helping me grow with the creative power of His being. In the stillness of the early morning, I feel His warmth and light awakening me, pushing away the shadows of my body-consciousness, charging the battery of truth within me. His power shines into my being, protecting, guiding, and strengthening me.

When I focus on God as the spiritual Mother, I am empowered by a flow of love, mercy, and acceptance that is unconditional and unending. In this relationship, God personifies the feminine principle, nurturing with tenderness and care, able to give constantly without any other agenda. This Supreme Mother also forgives, enabling me to learn from my mistakes. It's beautiful to go to God as the Mother in the evening, put the day in front of Her, feel Her acceptance and guidance, and become free from all burdens.

TEACHER

It is central to God's role that He has a deep desire to share all He knows. Particularly at this time, it's as though the Supreme, like a ripe seed, is bursting to give human beings the benefit of the truth He holds.

Very consciously, I can draw on a relationship with God as my Supreme Teacher to obtain nourishment for the mind and maintain my spiritual growth. This can come through silent connection in meditation and also through my own efforts to put into practice the main lesson, that of recovering and maintaining awareness of myself as a soul in relationship with God.

It's good to set aside the ego of thinking I am already grown up and don't need to learn any more. Such thinking makes the mind stagnant and leaves me open to wasteful or negative thought. Instead, when I think of myself as a student, my mind stays fresh and enthusiastic. Setbacks become learning opportunities. God the Teacher helps me understand what is going on in the world around me so that I can interpret it constructively and deal with it successfully.

I don't receive knowledge alone but the strength to keep moving along the path to a point where I can truly become wise. In meditation, knowledge comes to me from within, and I realize that I can become the embodiment of that knowledge if I let go of habits of thought or feeling that contradict it. God, the Truth, helps me move toward that state of truth.

COMPANION AND GUIDE

During the day, it's beautiful to keep God as my friend, companion, and guide. The relationship one has with friends can be even more intimate than the relationship with family.

One can't choose one's parents, but one certainly chooses one's friends. When I choose God as my closest friend, my mind will be drawn in the direction of that companionship because it's something I appreciate, value, and enjoy. In success and failure, in moments of happiness or when I face difficulties, in victory and defeat, I can keep my sense of perspective by sharing everything with my spiritual friend. God will also serve me as a truly impartial guide.

In any situation in which I am uncertain how to move forward, I connect for a moment with the Supreme, the One who has absolute truth. Then the question to ask is not what do I want or what do others want, but this: What does God want?

The deeper my connection has been with God in meditation, the clearer the answer has come. It's also a matter of practice, just as sometimes you have to grow accustomed to someone's voice to be able to understand that person. When I have learned to listen to God accurately, it's as if there's a whisper in my ear: I'll know, without wasting time and energy, the right course of action.

AT THE END OF THE DAY

So much happens in the course of each day, it is enormously valuable, before I go to sleep at night, to come into God's presence, review the day's highlights, and as far as possible settle the accounts.

In many professional areas of life today, people recognize the need for reflection and audit to maintain and improve both the service to clients and the job satisfaction of service providers. Checking my own behavior as a daily discipline enables me to continue to develop and grow as a human being and in the quality of my work and relationships.

Putting my day before the Supreme with real humility, I'll find I am helped to see clearly where there has been progress and where I failed. God's truth illuminates my life with accurate judgment but also with benevolence, and so I learn. God the friend is with me, wanting to lead me to perfection.

I want to fulfill my side of these relationships, and so I recognize where I must change and what I must do to make good any damage for which I have been responsible. Where my actions have been powerful, I'll be aware that the strength behind them came from my living relationship with the Supreme, and there will be neither worry nor complacency but only love and contentment in my dreams.

CREATOR AND CREATION

To describe a relationship with so elevated a being as God by using terms such as Mother, Father, and Friend might sound overfamiliar to some. These terms are not meant to be taken lightly, however. They describe different meditation experiences available to us with which we can experiment at different times of the day, going into silence and focusing on God.

Genuine communication with God requires commitment, respect, and cleanliness of spirit. These are prerequisites for an accurate connection. Given this accuracy and the concentration and stability that go with it, meditation opens channels of communication with the divine that help God's benevolent purposes to be served.

Although we describe experiences of God in terms of human relationships, the Supreme Soul is not, of course, limited by a human body. However, we cannot usefully say that God is everywhere, in all souls and even in matter, as some traditions maintain.

Instead, Raja Yoga meditation works with the very powerful concept that all souls, including the Supreme, retain their unique existence and identity eternally. Rather than thinking that God is a part of me or that I am part of

God, it's useful to understand that there is always a difference between the two, although we are intimately related.

Whereas human souls fluctuate in the expression of their qualities, God, the Absolute, is unchanging and retains positive attributes to an infinite degree. Recognition of this difference between the soul and the Supreme forms the basis of the love that pulls the soul to God in meditation. It's why we want and need the relationship. It helps us recover our truth.

Human souls reflect God's qualities, just as in a painting the qualities of the artist shine through. We can become the image of God's qualities. We can even aspire to become one with God and have that experience of oneness. Yet there will always be a difference between Creator and creation.

As in any play, not all the actors in the eternal play of existence are on stage at the same time. When we are offstage, it is as though we are resting, in a dimension beyond the physical. As eternal soul, however, we keep our individuality even when we are no longer wearing the costume of the physical body. Although we are not enacting our roles at that point, the totality of our part remains merged in the soul, in a highly compressed form, waiting for the time when it will be expressed again on the stage of the world.

God's role is also unique. As the eternal Seed, the unchanging point of reference for all that is highest in humanity, He is a living Source of the highest qualities. In meditation, it is more accurate and empowering to think of God as this divine Source than as an omnipresent energy. We remain aware that we have consciously to connect to the Source.

My meditation is more powerful when I keep in mind the distinction between God the living Seed of the human family and the family of souls who make up the human world. But it is also my right, as well as my responsibility, to enjoy a relationship of love and respect with the Supreme. By rekindling the awareness of my eternal self as a bodiless being and remembering the Father who is always without a body, I'm able to reclaim a state of purity, peace, and happiness that probably never left my innermost ideals but seemed out of reach in this imperfect world. Another useful understanding in Raja Yoga is that God is not omnipotent in the sense of being able to exercise an arbitrary authority outside nature's laws.

Neither the soul nor the Supreme Soul is "supernatural." Souls are a part of the natural world, of the way things are within the eternal drama of existence, albeit a wonder of nature whose reality is revealed to us by God rather than through the methods of science.

God, however, creates neither the stage of the world nor the play that is enacted upon it. One of the wrong ideas that alienated us from Him was to blame Him for natural disasters or for those of our own making.

Much that is happening in today's world is definitely not according to God's will. Rather, it is according to human possessiveness and desires. Were it not so, there would be the question of why a God whom we rightly think of as compassionate and merciful should be allowing so much suffering. The idea of an all-powerful God does not fit the reality of our experience.

God is our Beloved. His act of creation is actually to re-create us, decorating us with all His qualities, when we understand Him properly and stay in loving remembrance of Him.

TUNING IN

Powerful human personalities can spread their influence far beyond the place where they happen to be situated physically. But for that to happen, others need to be attuned to their feelings and will.

In the same way, the Supreme Soul, whose home is in a region of light, beyond physical dimensions, nevertheless does have the authority and power to influence events in the physical world. As the Supreme Benefactor, however, God can only bring benefit to the world. Furthermore, human minds must become attuned to God's will for this benefit to be enacted.

Through meditation, renewing my connection with the divine, I realize that I am able to share in the task of creating a better world. Human actions created today's conditions, and, if we choose, human actions will transform the world.

God will provide the power, wisdom, love, and strength to bring about these changes, but we have to make a deliberate decision to give our minds to God in order to take that power.

Meditation allows me to attune my mind to God's mind. The metaphor of a radio transmission is quite apt. Broadcasts from a radio station reach in all directions invisibly, but only receivers adjusted to the particular frequency are able to catch the transmission.

Similarly, God is in one location, the region of light beyond the physical world, but God's attributes are available to each of us, everywhere, when we tune to the right wavelength.

However, the relationship between souls and the Supreme is more intimate than the analogy of a broadcast allows. God's home, the region of light, is also the home of souls. We come from the region beyond to play our parts on the world stage, and even though we may forget this, God does not. God may not be omnipresent or omnipotent, but as the Supreme Parent, God has a mind that is all-encompassing, knowing each of the children personally.

We have our individual parts to perform, but ultimately God knows the state of play in every corner of the world stage. When the suffering brought on by our loss of truth becomes widespread, when we reach the point where the darkness has caused us to stumble so much that we are crying out for light, the Supreme Light comes. With unlimited love and respect, God puts us back on our feet and tells us how to stay that way.

Even then, it is still we human beings who have to draw on the Light by consciously making the link with God. We definitely have a special responsibility.

A JOURNEY THAT TRANSFORMS

It is in the nature of the soul to express itself, and of course, the main way the soul does this is through the body. When we hold on to an awareness of the spiritual dimension while playing our parts on the physical stage of the world, life is rewarding. Our actions come from a place of truth and are truly satisfying.

When we lose sight of the spiritual dimension, everyday activities begin to become burdensome and we lose our creativity and sense of play. At first, we try to make up for that loss by playing the game of life harder, looking for ever bigger doses of stimulation through the senses. While that remains our strategy for striving after happiness, mention of God is likely to provoke a yawn.

However, those who are ready to get to know God through meditation have a fascinating journey in front of them. The experience is of having a very rich character come into my life. The relationship is ever fresh because I am constantly seeing new facets of God's personality emerge before me. This also keeps me wondering what is going to be revealed next.

God's form is so simple—just a point of light. Yet, like a hologram containing a recording of all that is, that light contains an immense volume of experience so that even a lifetime's exploration does not bring you to the limits of knowing God. The more you dive into the ocean of knowledge contained within the light, the more you discover and the more treasures of knowledge and experience you receive. Thus, once this journey of exploration and discovery has started, there's a great incentive to continue.

I have also found that every time I make contact with God, something shifts within me. It's just as if I've been on a journey, after which I'm never quite the same again. However much time I spend in God's company in meditation, whether it's five minutes or an hour, there's always movement and growth.

The deepest experience of God comes as an affair of the heart. Making the connection in meditation, however, can be an entertaining and inventive task for the intellect. Here are some examples of ways of thinking about the Supreme that can help both mind and heart link with God and appreciate to the full the treasures received.

The Gardener

What are the foremost qualities of a gardener? Perhaps patience, tirelessness, vision, and a good sense of balance top the list. Gardeners give time and consistent attention to the plants in their care. They try to ensure that the plants receive water, food, sunshine, and shade in the right amounts and that they are protected against being swamped by weeds or destroyed by pests.

Given this care, the plants grow healthily. They blossom and bloom and are able to bear fruit. A beautiful garden can emerge where previously there was a jungle of weeds and thorns. In the same way, God tends every human soul and nurtures it with such patience and skill as to restore its full potential. God showers us with truth, warms us with love, and shows us how to weed out wasteful thoughts and how to protect ourselves against adverse influences.

We come to God feeling like thorns, prickly, hurting others and ourselves through anger, greed, or egotistical behavior that has grown out of control. God accepts us exactly as we are and with tireless love, patience, and positive vision teaches us what we need to know to transform into a wonderful garden of flowers.

With meditation and spiritual study, we obtain the fullest measure of God's care, protection, and transformative power. Filled with divinity, our original natures are revealed, and thorns fall away. We become able to share with others the fragrance and beauty of the truth that the Master of the Garden never stops seeing in us.

> *Sitting quietly, turning inward, I think of the Being of Light . . . the One who is Supreme in love and peace, purity, wisdom, and joy . . . In the presence of the Supreme I feel the comfort and security of being surrounded by God's light . . . I stay connected with this light, and it's as though God's truth, God's mercy, is reaching the roots of my being, making me strong . . . and as I feel the warmth of God's love, my heart opens . . . I become able to share fragrance and beauty with the world.*

The Goldsmith

To remember God as the Goldsmith and Jeweler is to invite total purification of the soul. A real jeweler doesn't like artificial materials. He'll obtain pure gold from low-quality alloy by heating the metal in a furnace. Furthermore, he doesn't want to see a single flaw—he knows how much it reduces a precious stone's value.

Meditation is like a fire of purification. I put myself into

God's care with love and humility, knowing this is the way to bring out the best in me. God the Goldsmith makes sure that all the impurities, the false and artificial aspects of my personality, are removed.

Courage and faith are needed to undergo this transformation, because there comes a point where the metal has lost its previous form but hasn't yet been reshaped into something new. I may find myself in a fluid, formless in-between state, neither one thing nor the other.

I have let go of the support my previous identity and position gave me and haven't yet developed the new role I would like to play. I am also more aware than ever of the rubbish mixed in the soul as it separates out from that which is real and true in me.

As soon as I say I want to change, it's a challenge to the forces of negativity, within and without, to come and test me. At such times, complete faith in the craftsmanship of the Supreme is needed. I know that I am in God's skillful hands and that the process will produce something of great value. The challenge is simply to stay still.

> *The intensity of my love for God increases . . . It becomes like a fire, cleansing the soul . . . I realize that I had*

accumulated so much impurity, so much that was negative
and artificial . . . The fire draws this out of me, and
it leaves me . . . I let go of physical aspects of identity,
knowing these are, in any case, impermanent . . . It feels
like I have nothing, but I see that I am becoming light
and free from burdens . . . God's love is purifying
me . . . I emerge from the fire as pure gold . . . Staying
in the hands of the Jeweler, as a child of God, I know
that my original beauty is being restored.

The Boatman

Religious and literary texts have often used the image of a
boat journey as a metaphor for transformation. Casting one's
boat from the shore means letting go of old certainties in
hopes of finding something new and better. Meditation
allows me to see very clearly what is on the other side of the
water.

Turning within, experiencing God's qualities, and realizing my own potential, I develop a vision of a place of love,
truth, and happiness, a place without pain. This gives me the
strength to entrust my life to God as the Boatman. I feel that
come what may, I'm ready to leave the shore of the old world,
without looking back.

When I put myself in God's boat, I am making a decision that will be difficult and perhaps dangerous to try to reverse. The boat won't sink no matter how much I rock it, but if I fall out, others might follow. If I try to swim back to the shore I left behind, I may drown. The journey is one only I can choose. No one can push me onto it or pull me off it. I look at the options and come to my own decision.

God's boat is the boat of knowledge. When I sit in it, I don't physically leave the world around me, but I step away mentally and emotionally. I look at the old world through different eyes. I see it through the eye of knowledge, of spirituality. I can no longer be engrossed in its temporary satisfaction, its false goals and cheap dreams. I have my eye on a new horizon.

As the boat reaches the middle of the ocean, storms may come, but I maintain the trust that the Boatman knows what he is doing. It's a new experience for me but not for Him. He has done it innumerable times before, and He knows exactly what needs to happen.

I can help by ensuring harmony and unity with fellow passengers. They have all had the courage to make the conscious choice to sit in the same boat. The love and respect I show them will help them maintain faith in themselves. We are all to reach the goal at the same time. Faith in the boat, faith in the Boatman, faith in the other passengers—combined, these help maintain faith in the self so that I pass whatever storms may come. After the storms, calmer weather follows in which the destination becomes clear again and the boat moves forward with ease.

I look back on the life stretched behind me and appreciate my fortune . . . I see the richness of the experience I have received and of the lessons learned . . . and now it is time to move on . . . place myself with God, the Boatman, in the boat of knowledge, the boat of truth . . . I am aware of the care, strength, and wisdom of the Boatman . . . His power enables me to leave behind my attachments and desires . . . In His company, experiencing His love and truth, I feel the old shore has been left far behind . . . and looking ahead, I see a place of truth, beauty, and love . . . I realize that my time with the Boatman is filling me with these qualities . . . I am becoming worthy to enter heaven.

The Sculptor

God has been remembered as the Sculptor. Again, it's my faith in the Sculptor's vision of his finished work, waiting to emerge from the block of wood or stone, that allows me to place myself in His hands. There is a spiritual beauty and perfection in me, as in every soul, hidden beneath layers of body-consciousness—the materialistic outlook I developed when my sense of who I am became tied to the body and the physical world.

When I meditate, I become aware of myself again as a spiritual being, and I am reminded of my original qualities. When I come in front of God, the vision of perfection is so clear that I feel I must regain my original condition.

Thus, I am able to trust the Sculptor, knowing that the knocks I receive will chip away at my weaknesses and restore my truth and beauty. I may not know myself or have full faith in myself, but God knows me and has full faith in me, and this knowledge gives me the strength and courage to stay put while the Sculptor continues his task.

I focus my thoughts on the Supreme, the being who is perfect, the Absolute . . . I feel loved . . . This love reminds me of the beauty there is within the self . . . I feel there is a vast difference between how God sees me and how I am at the present moment . . . I continue to hold God's vision of me and to keep myself in God's

hands . . . All the Sculptor wants of me is to be still . . .
When I keep my mind still, God's love and power
reshapes me, transforms me . . . that which is highest and
most beautiful in me begins to emerge.

The Director

"All the world's a stage, and all the men and women merely players." To take Shakespeare's words simply as metaphorical would be to lose the real depth of their meaning. When, through meditation, I go into the experience of myself as a soul, separate from the body, the idea of myself as an actor playing a part on the stage of the world becomes a living reality for me.

There is, then, also great power in connecting with God as the Director of the play we are enacting. It's a relationship that is particularly fruitful at this time, with more than six billion actors crowded onto the stage of the earth.

God's vision encompasses the entire drama: every twist and turn in the role of every actor, from past to present and future, from beginning to end and beginning again. Connecting my mind to God's, I am able to disconnect my energies from these closing scenes in which there is so much suffering and put my heart instead into rehearsing for the new beginning.

With the understanding and faith that scenes of great beauty are to appear in a short while, I learn from the Director how to play my own part accurately, precisely, and beautifully, now as well as in the future.

An actor who loses himself in the play or who wants to do things his own way will not be as successful as one who is willing to listen to and learn from the director. He'll get upset and confused. If I keep a little space between me and my role so that I don't lose sight of the Supreme Director's instructions and the way the play is moving, my part will be much easier to perform and better appreciated by all.

Remembering that I am an actor on the world stage, for a short while I put aside my costume and role . . . I, the soul, leave this stage, and with the power of my mind, I journey to my home, the region of light . . . In my home, I touch purity, peace, and happiness, and I feel my battery recharge . . . I look down to the stage and see much activity . . . There is comedy, tragedy, joy, suffering, heroism, upheaval . . . I step back onto the stage, but I maintain recognition of myself as an actor . . . I preserve my dignity and sovereignty as I play my role . . . I stay connected with the Director so that I can catch the signals he wants to give and understand where the play is going . . . Linked with the Supreme, I become peaceful, open, generous, and unlimited.

Trust and faith count for a great deal in a relationship with God. It isn't blind faith, though—more a matter of keeping vision and understanding clear.

Plants and trees benefit from the vision of the gardener as he digs and prunes long before seeing any flowers and fruits. Gold surrenders to the furnace and to the jeweler's tools in order to be molded.

When I put myself in God's boat, it is because I have glimpsed my transformed self. The marble yields to the sculptor, and the actor to the director, in order that a higher vision should prevail.

MY CONSTANT COMPANION

The meditation of Raja Yoga is a discipline of the mind that allows me to dwell on truth so that I am able to develop union with the Supreme. In an absolute sense, union implies inseparability, and it is certainly a goal in Raja Yoga that I, the soul, should become so free of limitation in my consciousness as to become at one with God.

The aim in Raja Yoga is not to lose myself in God, however, but to find myself. Meditation offers a means of developing such pure consciousness, through the relationship with God, as to allow me to transform. I want to receive so much truth from God as to be able to live according to my heart's deepest desire, with positivity and sovereignty. I want to say goodbye to fear and dependency and live like a carefree king.

Yet the world today, including my own nature, is far from perfect. So how is this possible? The answer is to keep God as my constant companion. While remaining clear in my mind that we are two, I want us to live and work together in the world as one. My desire is to bring God into the heart of my being, into the very center of my life. I'm not just going to experience God's qualities and develop the different relationships with God intermittently; I want to become like the Supreme.

Meditation is the means of validating, experiencing, and becoming the truth that spiritual understanding offers. When I experiment with the consciousness of myself as a soul, I can know myself as distinct from this body. That experience helps me regain control over my senses, my mind, my emotions, and my personality. I lost that control when I mistakenly identified myself with my physical reflection in matter—the body and its roles and relationships.

I also realize that in my state of purest potential, I share with God a home that is eternal, beyond time and space, a place of rest. Taking my mind to that region of divine light, I focus on the One who has all qualities, the Seed of the entire family of souls. I connect with that One so that God's living energy enters me, resonating with my own deepest truth, and I become renewed and transformed.

The more I receive from God, the easier it becomes to remember this Being with love, not just while sitting formally in meditation but through the whole day. It's the way a lover remembers her beloved except that there are no physical images involved: just the consciousness that I, the soul, belong to that One and that One belongs to me.

In this way, I get to know God, experience the joy of giving my heart and mind to the One, the peace that comes through freedom from selfish desires, and the happiness of being able to remind others of their own truth.

In deep meditation, God's love takes me into a beautiful, transcendent domain where there is a sense of an underlying unity within creation. However, I don't make the mistake of thinking God is everywhere or that I am God, as devotees have sometimes believed. Self-realization means knowing myself as an individual soul whose own unique, eternal part includes a time when I lose sight of the truth of my divinity as well as a time when I am able to live by it. This makes me constantly aware that I now have to reclaim that truth by consciously connecting to the Source, removing the negative tendencies within me.

Union denotes the idea of communication and, at a deeper level, communion. When I put my thoughts to God, I also allow my mind to be silent and still, because it is in silence that I can listen to what God has to say and know what I must do.

If I don't make that effort to connect and receive, a staleness of spirit will set in after the initial joy of accessing the transcendent domain. I won't be able to understand why my meditation has lost its depth and sparkle. It's as if I have cheated in a game—ending it, in fact, by turning the two players into one. I'll remain unclear about how to be a true instrument for God. Knowledge of the uniqueness of every soul allows me to see my fellow humans with the same benevolent eyes that God sees them with—each one a divine spark, a child of God, but with its own distinctive part to play. When I take my mind beyond the physical, I experience this entire, unlimited family of human beings as my brothers. Those with whom I come into contact receive a feeling of God as warmth and acceptance grow in me, reflecting the love and understanding God feels toward us all.

3 | RELATIONSHIPS

MEDITATION AND COMMUNICATION

Meditation charges the battery of the soul, making available a positive energy that increases my capacity for creating positive and fruitful connections and relationships with others. Connecting my mind with God is like plugging into a main electricity supply. The energy received vertically from the Supreme Being—unlimited peace, love, purity, wisdom, and joy—flows out horizontally into my actions and relationships.

The love and wisdom I receive from God enable me to love, know, and understand myself. The sense of God's pure good wishes enables me to respect myself. Communication with God answers my questions about myself and brings me peace and fulfillment. When I communicate with others from this stable space, it is as though my meaning is carried on a wave of goodwill, easily reaching the other person or persons. The meeting of minds precedes the transfer of meaning! In contrast, communication is difficult when I don't like and understand myself. My confusion and lack of self-respect trigger confusion in others.

CLEANLINESS OF ATTITUDE

The light of meditation brings clarity to the self, about the self. This helps me communicate much more clearly than I can when I am not sure what is going on inside me. Effective communication promotes understanding and strengthens relationships. More important, relationships are also connected with attitude and vision. Sometimes I may feel I have said and done the right things, yet still someone is not behaving toward me as I would wish. It is valuable at such times to check my attitude toward that person and the vision with which I am seeing him. I may find a slight feeling of disapproval, a resistance to something in his personality. Neither of us may be conscious of it, but this feeling casts a shadow on the other person. That person is not receiving the acceptance or respect that he should, and that influences his ability to hear me and the way he behaves toward me.

The discipline of meditation enables me to clean out my thoughts, feelings, and attitudes, ensuring that what I share with others is positive. Then it is much easier for others to connect with me in a positive way.

POWER OF POSITIVITY

Meditation also transforms my responses to others. As I remember that I am an eternal soul, a child of the Supreme Soul, I fill with God's love and peace. My original qualities, present in every soul in its pure state, are brought to the fore, and where previously there would have been conflict, I have a greater capacity to remain peaceful in the face of another person's unpleasant behavior.

This power to stay mentally and emotionally stable in the face of provocation makes me master of my fate instead of a slave to the other person's negativity. It is enormously valuable in life, enabling me to cool volatile situations and even remove another person's anger altogether.

Seeing past the anger on a person's face to the nonphysical, starlike being within also increases my power. This happens in a natural way when, through my meditation, I am actively aware of the spiritual bond all human beings share as souls who have a common origin in the One. With generosity of spirit, I connect with the goodness in the soul, knowing this to be a deeper reality than the anger. The wonder is that if I can hold this soul-conscious vision steady long enough, it awakens the goodness within the other person. Then peace really does prevail.

POSSESSIVENESS AND DEPENDENCY

Close personal relationships offer some of the biggest challenges to our ability to sustain peace and positivity. This is connected with the fact that family intimacy, though capable of being a source of inspiration and joy, can also bring about possessiveness and dependency. These are widespread diseases of the spirit in today's world but can be cured by meditation.

A telltale symptom of these diseases is lack of courtesy. Our nearest and dearest become victims of behaviors we would not dream of showing toward people with whom we are less familiar. It's not just a question of manners but of respect.

So often, a hierarchy of relationships becomes established in which, for example, the father takes it for granted that he will be listened to by the mother—or vice versa. Or an older brother orders around a younger family member, not giving the sibling space in which to speak his or her own mind. Once established, these patterns tend to be carried with us through life so that even when we have left the original family setting, we bring the same tendencies into our new relationships.

Meditation brings a very different element into the picture. As I become aware of myself as an eternal soul, an actor on the stage of the world, the realization grows that the role I am playing with others now is only one part of the whole.

I don't know where I was before I took this birth or where I will be afterward. The same is true for those with whom I am close. I do have a particular responsibility toward them while we are playing our parts together, but this lasts only a short time within eternity. As husband and wife, for example, each person has a particular role today, but who knows about yesterday or tomorrow?

In meditation, I stabilize in the consciousness that I am an eternal soul and that all human beings are souls, members of a huge, all-embracing family. Roles will change, but as souls we are brothers—we have no other relation. When I bring this consciousness into family life, it provides a positive and secure foundation for everyday interactions. Renewing the awareness of eternal truths protects against limited feeling of "my" husband, "my" wife, "my" son, and so on, where such feelings signify possessiveness and a desire to control rather than family unity and loyalty.

I still have my own unique role to play, but misunderstanding and suffering are reduced when the part in me that tries to control others or that abandons control to others is left behind. Both of these are essential negative behaviors, born of insecurity, not true responsibility or love.

When I know myself as a soul in relationship with the Supreme, my self-respect returns. There is an inner detachment and the feeling that here on the stage, I, the soul, am alone—it is just a role that I play here with others. From this strong vantage point, I'll no longer feel a need to manipulate others but instead will bring pure feelings of genuine love and appreciation into my relationships.

INNER FREEDOM

The experience of meditation is of I, the soul, becoming absolutely detached from the physical realm, completely free, self-sufficient, and independent. One of the purposes of meditation is to taste this inner freedom. When I come into relationship with others with this consciousness, I do not make demands of them as I might otherwise have done, because I am full. I play a role, and there is interaction, but I do not impose on others, and my connections are that much more harmonious and beautiful.

There's a simple equation expressing a mistake commonly made in our most intimate relationships: $\frac{1}{2} \times \frac{1}{2} = \frac{1}{4}$. When I give my heart to another or conquer someone's heart, feeling that I am only half a person without him or her and that the two of us coming together will make a whole, it rarely works. After the initial romance, what usually happens is that instead of complementing one another, we lean on each other. Over time, this weakens us, and along with the positive feelings that remain, we start to irritate each other. Eventually, our love may become mixed with hate so that we clash with each other in frustration.

Thus, our energies are not multiplied but become much reduced. The difference, if I'm a mediator, is dramatic. As

I learn to connect with God's energy of truth, I can take all that I need to become whole, filling myself completely with whatever was missing. Having filled myself, I come into action and interaction with others from a position of giving rather than one of needing to take.

LOVE, RESPONSIBILITY, AND ATTACHMENT

When I experience detachment from the pull of the physical realm, I can link to the Source. While my consciousness is attached to my body and bodily relationships, I can't make that contact. The detachment I need to experience is one in which my sense of who I am is spiritually oriented so that body-consciousness no longer binds me and I can make the connection with God through which I am filled with love. Then the love that I bring to my partner or others close to me becomes deeper and more genuine than before, bringing an exchange of goodness and happiness rather than dependency. In all my relationships, my ability to give increases.

Love, responsibility, and attachment are often confused with one another. Attachment is recognizable by the grief it causes. It is actually an opening for pain. It causes me to cling to someone, to try to hang on to her even when she wants the space to fly free. The more I do this, the greater the pain I store up for myself, because I cannot hold on to anything forever other than my own unique identity as a soul.

When I have attachment, I lose sight of my true responsibilities. Because attachment causes me to seek to take from others, it blinds me to how to give appropriately.

STEPPING BACK

A mother may know what is good for her child in terms of diet and nutrition, but because of her attachment, she may be unable to refuse the child's requests for junk food. She knows yet another sugary indulgence will probably make the child fractious and hyperactive later and unwilling to eat food that is more nutritious. But when attachment takes over, she forgets her responsibility to ensure a balanced diet. The mother can't resist the immediate pleasure of seeing her child enjoying another ice cream.

That is a relatively small matter, perhaps, but the same principle extends in many different directions. Because of my attachment and my desire for praise or approval from the objects of my attachment, I may forgo certain responsibilities at many levels—at home and at work, toward my community, and toward humanity in general.

Soul-consciousness helps me overcome such tendencies, which can make me lazy. I am able to step away from these attachments and see more clearly what I need to do. In fact, the greatest and most worthwhile service I can perform is periodically to step back from the world stage, remembering myself as a soul, and my eternal resting enables me to drop the illusions that develop when I become too engrossed in events on the stage, so that I'm automatically able to play my role in the right way.

LOVE WITHOUT PAIN

A sign of genuine love in relationships is that I will neither feel pain nor cause others to feel pain. Real love means no exchange of pain, only an exchange of happiness. This is so different from common perceptions, in which love is confused with attachment and the pain of loss is never far away.

Real love widens the scope of my life enormously. It means I can be with someone and love them and receive love, but if circumstances change and I'm no longer with them, there won't be sorrow. We'll both be free to move on to the next scenes in our lives as the need arises.

Love means an exchange of happiness, because we are able to give. Love means we are able to bring each other closer to God and grow in that way too. Love brings cooperation in which I am able to see others as souls playing their roles on the stage without getting hooked into expectations of how they will perform.

Love enables me to maintain inner independence while performing my own role so that I can see what really needs to be done and not just react to immediate pressures.

GIVING AND TAKING

In every human exchange, there's a giving and taking involved, but it isn't always clear which is which. This is the case because the real exchange is at the level of the impact on consciousness rather than at a physical level.

The mother who gives in, because of her own attachment, to her child's demands for another ice cream is actually taking something from that child, and in return she'll just get more bad behavior. In contrast, when a mother cares for a child from her heart and gives the love and attention that the child needs to develop well, there will be a rich return of love, loyalty, and affection.

The actions we perform in relation to others will always have consequences, but whether the impact is positive or negative will depend on motivation and circumstances. For example, if it is a wife's genuine joy to prepare a special lunch for the family on Sundays, everyone will be appreciative. If, however, her underlying motive is to stop her husband from spending so much time out with his friends on the golf course, she'll be enraged when he comes in late. And he'll most likely be late the next time.

Relationships enter a state of crisis when there is an imbalance of giving and taking. If a husband is demanding but unappreciative, his wife may carry on meeting those demands for years, but eventually she'll probably ask herself, What's in this for me? At that point, the relationship may break down, or there may be a complete change in its dynamics in which the wife dictates her own terms for its continuation. Literally, she seeks to get her own back on her husband—her own independence, the self-respect she had given away.

Meditation acts as a catalyst for change in such circumstances but helps ensure a positive outcome rather than revenge and recriminations. I've seen dramatic changes in personalities and behavior thanks to meditation. A domineering individual, awakening to the sweet experience of the consciousness of the soul, begins to become humble and respectful instead of egotistical and controlling. As the spiritual hunger inside that person reduces, so his or her demands on others, physical as well as emotional, become less pressing.

One who had previously played the part of a victim discovers that in the genuine humility that accompanies soul-consciousness, there is respect for others but also a great authority that will not permit him or her to be disadvantaged any longer. Humility, properly understood, is a virtue, which means it is a strength. It does not seek to impose on others, but neither does it permit others to impose on the self, let alone obliterate the self.

Raja Yoga meditation makes me self-sovereign, not a supplicant. From that position of strength, I am better able to be more giving in my relationships at every level.

AN INVISIBLE CURRENCY

The give and take in our actions and relationships is known in the East as karma. Although the currency of this exchange is invisible, we can think of our relationships as entailing investment and withdrawals, as in a bank account or a business. If I withdraw more than I invest, there will be trouble.

For example, an executive is traveling a lot and his secretary deals with a huge amount of work while he is away. Instead of acknowledging how much his success depends on her loyalty and accuracy and the responsibility she is fulfilling, he remains obsessed with his sales figures. Such a situation can go on for only so long. Usually, there will come a moment when, after so much has been given, the lack of appreciation becomes intolerable. The loyal worker will suddenly quit, perhaps leaving chaos in her wake.

Appreciation, to an accountant, means an increase in the value of assets. In the same way, appreciation within relationships increases their durability and value. It's a positive energy that when invested well adds to our stock of that invaluable asset—goodwill.

How would meditation affect this scenario? When we make the right connection with the divine, we are able to draw on unlimited stocks of goodwill. This produces a generosity of spirit from which appreciation of others radiates as a natural consequence. If the boss had been a meditator, he would not have become so disrespectful and unfeeling.

And the secretary? It might seem paradoxical, but meditation, by helping her maintain her self-esteem internally, would free her boss's love and appreciation. Her attitude would be that she was doing the work for her own satisfaction and for the feeling that what she was doing was right and must bring its own return in its own time.

If at some point her boss were suddenly to recognize what a jewel she was and change his behavior toward her, that would of course be fine. She wouldn't be begging for it, but her patience and tolerance would increase the chances of its happening. If she decided there was a better use of her time and energy elsewhere, that would also be fine. She would leave according to her own standards of decent behavior, without an outburst of rage or the wish for recrimination. But for as long as the job still suited her, she might decide to stay put rather than be pushed into quitting—perhaps into a worse situation—by feelings of resentment and frustration.

Meditation helps us keep our cool, greatly increasing the chances that we will judge situations correctly and act in ways

that build a good future rather than destroy what we have
already earned.

BREAKING NEGATIVE CYCLES

Sometimes, in close relationships at work or in the home,
a cycle of reactivity develops in which a person's habits or
personality traits become a source of chronic irritation to me.
Instead of simply accommodating the other person's nature,
I find myself needled by it repeatedly. Such bad feeling soon
reaches the other person, and a bond of negativity develops
between us. It grows stronger every time I react. Irritation
becomes dislike becomes anger, causing hurt on both sides.

Meditation enables me to break this vicious circle. By
giving me an opportunity to step back, it allows me to identify what I have been doing. With an understanding of the
damage caused by my reaction, I resolve to stop. At first,
perhaps, the best I can manage is not to strike out with words
even though I'm still getting worked up inside. Even that
degree of control will take the heat out of the situation.

As I continue to draw on God's love and peace, I'll develop
the power to change the quality of my thoughts and feelings as

well. Eventually, I'll remove the defect in my own character that was at the root of my reaction so that what used to needle me so much will now be water off a duck's back. That will also allow me to communicate my point of view in a nonoffensive way.

This is meditation at its most magical. I'll not only have removed a source of pain, I'll have grown spiritually as well. The person whom I was in danger of making into an enemy has become my teacher and friend!

Sometimes it's useful to let your thoughts go to the person with whom you have a difficulty and consciously send that person feelings of lightness and goodwill. This also helps cool a difficult situation.

Another healing strategy is to recognize that each of us has a mixture of strengths and weaknesses and to focus on appreciating the other person's strengths. Practiced consistently, such appreciation makes it easier for others to see what they need to do to change. But the primary impact is on me, in keeping me free of negativity.

Once, when I was reacting to a colleague, a senior yogi warned me that I was creating a negative bond with that person that would interfere with my relationship with God. I definitely didn't want that to happen. She then suggested that I look at the special strengths of that individual and asked me whether I would be able to do my job without her help—whether I could do the job they were doing. That made me stop and think. There was no way I could. I realized that in any task you need many talents to come together and that I mustn't criticize or demand that others change. What I can do is change myself, and learn to accept and appreciate others.

If my eyes are open to who I am, I am more likely to appreciate others and their qualities. Through my meditation, experiencing inner peace and seeing that I have a good relationship with God and am moving forward well, I feel a contentment that makes me much more amenable to other people. I am less likely to find fault, criticize, complain, demand, or impose.

Most people are very discontented, which is what makes them critical of others. Then their critical outlook further alienates them from others, and so they become even more discontented.

Again, meditation gives me the creative energy to break this vicious circle. When I focus my thoughts on God, the love and happiness I feel through that contentment represent an attainment that does not depend on anybody or anything. I have it, and it is with me constantly while I keep open my line to the divine.

When a rough stone finds itself in a mountain stream, the water soon erodes it to the point where the sharp edges are gone. Like mountain water, good feelings seem soft and sweet, but they are also very powerful when maintained consistently. They will remove my own rough edges over time and do the same for others if I continue to do what I know is right. I just have to maintain the flow by keeping connected.

The stronger I become in receiving from God, the more of God's power I'll have available in my relationships, and this will automatically help others. Even if someone is behaving outrageously toward me, if I don't react but instead maintain a positive attitude and vision toward that person, constantly investing, there will come a moment of transformation when that person will say: You have put up with all this nonsense from me for so long, and really, I do appreciate it, and I think I need to change.

> *I let myself sit quietly so that I can have a few moments to reflect on what is happening . . . I take a deep breath and find that this focuses my attention inside . . . I can feel my body relax and the tension in my shoulders, my neck, and my face melts away.*

*And now I go inside. There's a recording within of the
action and interaction I've been involved with not just
for the past twenty-four hours but even for many days
or months . . . As I rewind this tape, I see powerful
memories . . . Sometimes the connection has been a sweet
one . . . sometimes the interaction hasn't been as I would
have wished . . . sometimes I was a little impatient, and
sometimes it really wasn't my fault at all.*

*But now, as I look back and reflect, I ask myself the
question: What next? Where do I want to go? And a
very clear vision emerges in front of me . . . I want to move
to that state of freedom where all the interaction I am
engaging in is filled with truth, with love, with sweetness,
without dependency, without possessiveness, without any
negative influences . . . I would like to come to that state of
freedom and truth . . . that really is my goal now.*

*I understand that in order to do this, I need to do
something about my own inner world . . . I have to create
a state of contentment, a state of fullness, in which all
that I need comes to me from one Source, the One up above,
the Divine, the Supreme . . . I realize that if I can do*

*this as all my needs are fulfilled, I will no longer go
searching here and there to find that fulfillment.*

*I begin this journey to fill myself, to reach that state of
contentment and fullness from the Source of love and peace,
from the Source of joy and truth . . . I fill myself . . . This
love quenches my thirst . . . it fills all the empty spaces
within me . . . I continue to drink from the Source, and
as this pure love reaches the soul, I can feel the power and
truth within it . . . Whatever my weaknesses, whatever my
mistakes, they are not a factor . . . The love simply comes
pouring forth.*

*And the love fills me, and the love heals . . . The
healing power of God's love goes deep within the soul,
so that the pain of the past finishes . . . Memories of
injustice, memories of my mistakes and the mistakes of
others go through the process of healing . . . I can be at
peace with myself and at peace with others around me.*

*As the love fills, I begin to come to a state of appreciation
of the fortune of my life and of the friends and family
that I have . . . The love changes my vision and my*

perception of the past . . . I can now forgive, let go, forget,
and be filled with such love and happiness that I can
share this now with my family and friends . . . and even
beyond. I can be an instrument to allow the power of this
divine love to reach out and help all those in suffering
and in need . . . I become an instrument, clean and
clear, so that the rays of this love reach out to my entire
human family so that God's love can reach the world
and transform the world.

Keeping this connection, I come back to the present
situation, the here and now, the things I need to deal
with . . . but totally in this consciousness of being full,
so that I can give and don't need to take . . . In this
awareness, I play my role on the stage.

RECOVERING SELF-WORTH

In Raja Yoga meditation, we generally speak of God as the Mother and Father rather than simply Father or even Father and Mother. This follows the biological pattern, in which the first relationship a child has is with the mother and then with the father. But the real reason is that bathing in God's unconditional love as is mirrored by a mother's total love and acceptance of her child is a vital step on the journey of spiritual transformation.

Whereas a father tends to place certain demands on the child, especially as it grows older, a mother often just picks up the youngster who has come into the house dirty and, without thinking about it, cleans the child up and feeds him and puts him to rest. It's a spontaneous response of love. That's an ideal, of course, and although it does certainly exist in reality, our individual experiences of family relationships differ. But in the case of God, we are talking about an absolute ideal. When I come to the Supreme Parent, dirty and tired after playing in the dust of body-consciousness for so long, God doesn't challenge me, saying, Why did you do all this? or Why didn't you do that? God simply accepts me with total love. The experience in meditation, as I take steps to open myself to God, is of God surrounding me with love and filling me with that love.

As I continue, the thought comes that I've had so much love from God, I'd like to give something back in return. Because of the experience of love, I feel ready to change—to sacrifice my attachments for the sake of the higher truth God's love has rekindled in me. I find myself becoming worthy.

In that state of cleanliness and worth, I am able to face God in the role of the father. When the Father sees I am a worthy child, he knows I am capable of taking care of his inheritance.

And what is the inheritance? It is the highest form of happiness, a state in which my mind becomes like God's mind: expansive, knowledgeful, and blissful, immune to the factors that cause most people so much sorrow in today's world. In this I can be of immeasurable help to others.

Most of us, when we come to the path of spirituality, have a sense of unworthiness. Lacking self-esteem, we wonder how it is possible for us to love God or for other people—let alone God—to love us.

I felt like this myself, but I found that by coming into a state of peace through the practice of soul-consciousness, I could then feel the love of God the Mother reaching out like the rays of the sun, without conditions or demands. The love purifies, cleanses, and transforms until my self-respect returns and I feel able to let myself experience real happiness again.

Lack of self-esteem is such a widespread affliction, it's worth looking at how it arises. The root cause is our self-forgetting. We have lost sight of our real identity—spiritual beings having a human experience. In the confusion of coming into the consciousness of the body and believing that we are physical beings who just somehow happen to have developed a sense of self, there is no value for the self.

This lack of self-worth causes us to seek out relationships in which we are bolstered by those around us. It works for a while, but unless we grow within the relationship, there will come a time when we are demanding support and others are unable to give it. That will provoke a crisis in us.

Second, we have allowed ourselves to become trapped by a variety of habits or addictions that weaken the soul. For a time, like dependency in relationships, these behaviors seem to be helping us keep our act together, but they are actually eroding our character and, with that, our freedom of choice. When we recognize that we have become trapped, our self-worth plummets.

A third factor that makes it difficult to maintain self-worth is failure to align conscience with behavior. When my conscience tells me to act in a certain way but my behavior is repeatedly quite different, I'll suffer a lot of stress relating to my image of myself. Sometimes people try to resolve this dilemma by blunting their consciences, but that leads to more wrong action, which over time just deepens the problem.

A fourth factor is lack of a nurturing atmosphere, especially in childhood but also in adult life. It is a great strength for a child to grow up feeling the presence of the divine in an atmosphere of optimism and love. That is very much missing in most families and, indeed, workplaces today. Despite the wonderful qualities people still bring to family life, we cannot give as much as we would wish when we have cut ourselves off from the creative core of our being.

These are among the conditions that have enslaved us in a chronic lack of self-worth. In essence, I don't respect myself because I have moved away from basic truths in my life. Meditation sets me free by bringing me back to the awareness that I am an eternal soul, with peace as my original nature, and allowing me to feel the beauty, truth, and power in knowing myself as a child of God.

The practice of soul-consciousness also enables me to access the full spectrum of my own original qualities, and these qualities reemerge and develop in my life so that I am able to see my true value again. Meditation is time spent in reflection on aspects of truth. I use my intellect to engage with and explore truth. The more time I give to this journey of discovery, the greater the opportunity for me to absorb that truth and integrate it in my thoughts, words, and actions.

Meditation is a way of life in which the goal is the transformation of my consciousness, the way I think, and the way I use my energy and other resources. It is a healing and purifying process, doing for me what all the king's horses and all the king's men were unable to do for Humpty Dumpty: putting my fractured being together again.

TURNING QUALITIES INTO POWERS

An important aspect of God, remembered throughout history in all cultures and traditions, has been the concept of an Almighty Authority. The interpretation of this concept has been varied, however. Some have conceived a God who is fearsome, who punishes, who extracts a tooth for a tooth. That is very different from the experience of God in meditation as a benign, benevolent, merciful parent; as a teacher of absolute wisdom, but a wisdom that includes gentleness and compassion; and as one who has total humility, who is free from of the demands of ego.

Yet it is also the experience of the soul that God is the Almighty Authority, the source of all power and strength. When I meditate and connect with the Supreme, I come to a state of truth in which the combination of all the qualities of soul—peace, love, purity, wisdom, and happiness—fills me with power.

When I first communicate with the Supreme and God's qualities begin to influence me, I feel replenished by the experience. But beyond that, as I fill deeper, the energy of truth that enters me becomes a positive power that overcomes negativity in myself and others so that those I am connected with become better able to experience their own truth. This power also extends to my physical surroundings, transforming the atmosphere around me.

There are interesting spiritual parallels to the way the physical sciences distinguish between energy and power. In physical terms, energy is defined as the *capacity* for doing work, whereas work means making this move. Power is defined as the *rate of* doing work.

Similarly, we can look upon spiritual energy as our capacity for experiencing the original qualities of the soul. We all have this capacity, but to different degrees.

Spiritual power is then seen as the extent to which we put these qualities to work in our relationships. We bring about change through our power to remain in a state of truth in the face of the various tests that come. Our actions and relationships give us an opportunity to utilize the power we have accumulated.

The qualities of God experienced in meditation are also the original qualities of the soul, but the link with God is essential for their full power to be expressed. In fact, God, too, needs the connection with us, despite having these qualities to the highest degree, in order to exercise His power to restore truth to the world.

The following pages describe eight key spiritual powers in terms of their application in everyday life.

The Power to Withdraw

The aim of Raja Yoga meditation is to strengthen the character so much that situations that previously might have defeated us we now find easy to handle. Thus, the power to withdraw does not mean running away from life but the ability to find a safe space inside oneself even in the midst of life.

An image used to illustrate this power is that of the tortoise. When there is danger, the tortoise instantly goes inside its shell, which it carries with it everywhere. In the same way, when I am faced with negativity or active hostility, there is great strength in becoming introverted, even for a moment, so as to touch base with the point of peace inside my own being. In doing so, I find not only shelter but also stability, so that I protect myself from any hostile reactions on my part.

When I am too open to the world around me, it's as though the arrows of negativity that fly around can easily penetrate my being so that I lose my truth. What others say and do quickly affects me, and I become reactive. This causes a buildup of stress, and eventually burnout, which makes me feel my only option is to retire from the fray altogether. I don't want to react; I want to act with concern and reason and effectiveness. When I develop the habit of making a momentary withdrawal in situations of danger, I'm better able to achieve this. Turning within, I'm able to remember my line to the divine, the line of love, the line that fills me with peace and wisdom and good wishes. It's like an exercise: going inward, upward, and then outward. Doing this repeatedly through the day as a discipline as well as at times of danger, I'll keep moving forward with stability and strength.

To maintain this power, I have to put a high value on introversion. If I'm too extroverted, I'll become caught up in external circumstances and won't have the power to withdraw available to me at the moment of need.

The Power to Pack Up
On the path of meditation, I am a traveler, undertaking a magnificent adventure. I have to make some firm choices about what I will take with me. To pack up means to learn the lessons of the present and then to move on, letting the past be past. It means not carrying the baggage of the past into my present and future but traveling lightly from one

day to the next, keeping only what is most useful to me. That way, I'll enjoy the journey more and move faster in the direction of my choice.

I'll also be lighter in my relationships. The power to pack up enables me to fill each exchange I have with others with freshness and newness instead of allowing influences from past encounters to affect my attitude and behavior. When I carry emotional or intellectual baggage from the past into my present dealings with an individual, I don't give that person the opportunity to express himself freely: My attitude colors him with the paint of my previous experience. It is important to process the past and learn from experience but then finish it so that it does not block my view of how things are today.

Meditation helps me acquire that discipline of finishing negative and wasteful thoughts. As the habit of self-observation develops, it doesn't take long to understand how negative thoughts and feelings literally negate my central aim of re-emerging my true nature. Negativity drains the battery of the soul faster than anything else does.

As I progress on my spiritual journey, even thoughts that waste the precious resources of the mind come to be seen as an impediment. Turning a scene over in my mind repeatedly is an example of severe waste—it will rob me of the mental concentration and emotional stability I need to keep moving forward. Sometimes we do get stuck, like a broken record, in such mental grooves without realizing what we are doing.

The power of packing up means I recognize the damage caused by such waste and put an end to it. As I renew the awareness of myself as a soul in relationship with God, the needle of my attention is lifted above the groove, letting me come fully into the present.

I also learn to be selective in what I choose to remember or forget from the past. This is not dishonest; in fact, it is being honest to my task. Human beings in any case have highly selective memories. Not only do we see and understand differently, according to our individual interests and agendas, our attitudes and perception also determine the memories we choose to store.

Meditation enables me to exercise this option quite deliberately, picking up the scenes from the past that nourish me and help me move forward and rejecting memories that pollute my mind and slow me down.

The Power to Tolerate
Think of a tree, its branches laden with fruit. When a child throws a stone at it, it bends its branches low in an offering

of its sweet fruit. The child eats the fruit, becomes satisfied, and learns to treasure the tree.

This beautiful image of the power of tolerance contains several lessons. It shows me that if I am to achieve the same thing, I must become laden with the fruit of attainments from God. When I am filled with joy, love, wisdom, beauty, and peace, even when the stones of difficult circumstances come my way I'll still be able to respond creatively, with strength. If I'm empty, the stones will injure me, and I'll react with anger or fear.

I must also remove any dryness or hardness in my heart that may have developed as a result of injuries experienced in the past, when I did not have God with me. These will prevent me from bearing and sharing the unlimited fruit made possible by the company of the Supreme.

Real tolerance does not just mean putting up with a difficult situation and still counting how many times I have had to endure it. Tolerance means that no matter what stones come my way, I recognize that those throwing them are empty, and so I continue to share good things with them.

For most human beings today, if someone insults them, they'll immediately become angry or upset in return, and so nothing gets resolved. Those with a good character may be able to smile for a while, responding with patience, but repeated assaults will wear them down until the point comes where they will react. If, however, through my meditation, I am receiving unlimited power from God, my heart will remain open and I won't count how many times the other person has insulted me. This may sound like an impossible ideal. Meditation, however, makes the impossible possible. Experienced yogis who have developed a very deep personal relationship with God and keep the Supreme as their constant companion display just such a power. It's immensely worthwhile for all of us to move toward that goal.

True tolerance is made possible by openness and acceptance. It doesn't mean gritting my teeth and carrying on, come what may. Repression or suppression of my feelings can cause me all sorts of internal damage and end in an explosion that damages others too.

Real tolerance is a state in which, first, I have to be very clear about my own contribution to a difficult situation. If the difficulty is signaling a need for me to change my own behavior, I have to be open and responsive to that.

Second, real tolerance requires understanding and compassion toward others: knowing that at the deepest level, all people wish to live with love, peace, and happiness and that when we behave badly toward one another, it's because we are suffering from a loss of these qualities. That doesn't mean I have to invite another person to continue to insult me or deliberately expose myself to difficulties. But if I happen to be in a situation in which there is continual assault, understanding will contribute to my power to tolerate it and accept it or walk away from it in peace.

Third, real tolerance is that state of fullness that comes only through the relationship with God, in which there is no impact from the assaults other than to provoke a response of wanting to give, like the fruit tree. A culture of tolerance is actually a culture of forgiveness. When we move very far away from God, tolerance levels run low. The nature we express becomes that of wanting, taking, and needing rather than our original nature, which is giving.

The Power to Accommodate

Closely linked to tolerance, the power to accommodate means having a heart so big and generous that I am able to rise above all differences of character and personality, knowing that every actor in the enormous drama of existence has a unique contribution and role. Whereas tolerance heals wounds and removes hurts, accommodation accepts and values differences, observing them and ultimately subsuming them in love, as an ocean absorbs the rivers that flow into the sea. While completing my own part as a river, I also need to be aware of God as the Ocean of Love and the Ocean of Wisdom. When I enter this consciousness through meditation, the goodness of all creation becomes clear to me very naturally, and it is no effort for me to go beyond conflict and clashes of opinion.

The Power to Face

Situations arise in which it may not be enough to tolerate or accommodate but in which I need power to face up to unpleasant and perhaps very threatening realities. What we are talking about here, in effect, is courage.

Meditation helps enormously. First, the practice of the awareness of myself and others as eternal souls greatly reduces fear of death, an ever-present reality that we spend much time, money, and mental and emotional energy trying to avoid. If soul-consciousness is firm enough, I'll have the absolute conviction that when someone dies, it's not that they are no more, just that they have moved farther on their eternal journey.

This faith makes it much easier to face up to the departure of someone close to me. It also removes much or all of the fear I might otherwise suffer about leaving my own body. I'll still value my life greatly, probably even more than before, because of having the burden of fear removed. But I won't let concern for the body stop me from facing what I must.

Second, meditation makes it easier for me to oppose evil. It does this by allowing me to distinguish clearly between the actor and the action. When there is real understanding of the original qualities of every soul and so no hatred in my heart for anyone, it becomes possible to stand firm against wrongdoing.

There is a saying in the East that when evil is fought with evil, only evil can win. If the negative behavior I am opposing activates negative tendencies within my own personality, the fight will soon wear me out and I'm unlikely to be victorious. In fact, one of the factors that prevent us from facing difficult situations is fear of our own reactions.

With a clean heart, a clear understanding of good and evil, and connection with the divine, I am much more likely to have the faith and courage with which to stand up for what is right.

The Power to Discern

Meditation gives me a discerning eye—an ability to discriminate between truth and falsehood. It does this by taking me into a consciousness that overrides all the competing claims to truth—the ideologies and opinions, reasons and analyses, justifications and stories—that can be so confusing.

The image of discernment is the jeweler, who, with the help of his eyeglass, is sorting out real diamonds from false. Meditation opens my third eye, the eye of pure consciousness. When I look at the world through this eye, truth is not just an intellectual idea but an experience of the heart. When I think and act in ways that maintain and deepen this experience, I know I am moving in the right direction.

Conversely, I discover that thoughts and behaviors that cloud the experience are coming from falsehood, no matter how much I or others may try to justify them.

Thus, meditation gives me a reliable basis for discerning the value in different courses of action: Will this help me recover my truth or take me further into falsehood? Will it maintain the flow of love, peace, and happiness in my heart, or will it cause a blockage?

Previously, I may have been easily swayed by other people's demands and opinions or by illusory ways of thinking arising from my own negativity. Like a good lawyer, the intellect is very clever at arguing its case regardless of where the truth may lie.

But when truth is experienced in and from the heart, there is no arguing with it. Deeply experienced truth clears my mind of irrelevancies created by possessiveness, greed, desires, and ego. As I learn to create pure, positive thoughts and connect with the divine, it is as though a flow of clear, fragrant water gradually displaces the mud and rubbish in my intellect, enabling me to see reality again.

The Power to Decide

Sometimes I'm faced not so much with a choice between truth and falsehood as with having to balance competing aims or priorities in deciding on a course of action. There's huge value in getting this right, because poor judgment can entangle me in consequences from which it might take years to recover. If I'm deflected because of my attachments or desires, I'll lose my ability to decide accurately.

Understanding myself as a soul and keeping my heart full and free through my relationship with God puts me in the best possible position to judge correctly. I'll be like the statue of Justice wearing a blindfold as she carefully weights the evidence: Free from prejudice arising from superficial appearances, above the influence of situations and the emotions and opinions of others, perfectly centered, she is optimally placed to sense the right way forward.

The Power to Cooperate

In India, there is a saying that when everyone gave a finger of cooperation, the mountain of sorrow was lifted. If we look with open eyes at the world of today and at current social, financial, and environmental trends, it's clear that there is widespread suffering and sorrow, that it is likely to get worse, and that to remove it will be a task like lifting a mountain.

Meditation ignites a conviction that the task will be done. Although we have such different backgrounds, cultures, personalities, and so on, meditation takes us to a place of understanding from which it becomes easy to share our resources, work together, and give our own finger of cooperation to the task.

The way meditation achieves this is interesting. Look at the other side—at what prevents cooperation: It is ego, where I am in a state of self-aggrandizement, hungry for personal praise or fame, and not concerned about the team. In ego, I think I am the only one who knows, the one who is right. Ego kills cooperation.

Ego is closely connected to body-consciousness. An enormous "I and my" factor comes in when I think of myself as this body and lose sight of the soul. My race, my color, my gender, my physical appearance, my education, my family, my job, my position, my possessions—all these become part of the buildup of ego. Working with others who may at any moment challenge my ego with their own distinct agendas and needs becomes stressful.

The more I practice meditation and develop and live with the consciousness that I am a nonphysical soul, a being of light, the quicker the ego associated with all those physical factors melts away. Coloring myself with God's company, I see others as the children of God. I know myself as part of the family of human souls who have the same original qualities that I have. In soul-consciousness, there is no way I can feel superior to others, though I'll value their specialties. We are brothers—equal yet distinct.

In this consciousness, a natural humility develops, a genuine respect for each other. There is a strength and happiness in the awareness of being a child of God, but I'll see others as the same. There is neither the ego of feeling superior nor the inverted ego of an inferiority complex. I am not negating myself, I am recognizing the value of the self, but I'm also appreciating the value and qualities of all others around me. In that spirit of mutual respect, it becomes easy to work together.

The future of the world and the transformation of the planet actually depend on this transformation in each one of us, from ego and self-aggrandizement to humility, respect, and cooperation. Meditation, by lifting me beyond the factors that divide us, makes me deeply aware that we are one family, sharing one home, this beautiful planet, for which we have a common responsibility. In the awareness of where we are and to whom we belong, there also comes the recognition of what we as a family must do together.

> *Sitting quietly, I go within, and in this awareness of my own state of self-esteem . . . I know I am eternal, immortal, a creation of the divine . . . I am a child of the divine . . . Recognizing the value of my life, the value of the self, stable in the state of self-respect, I connect with the Supreme, the Being of Light, my Mother, my Father, my Friend, my Teacher, my Beloved, my Companion, my Guide . . . I focus on this infinite Being, the One who is the Almighty Authority . . . and from the Supreme, the love, the peace, the purity pours forth for me to absorb.*

> *And as I absorb these beautiful treasures from God, they awaken within my own being the same response . . . God's peace resonates with peace within me, and I can feel this peace . . . not just feeling calm and quiet but*

*peace becoming a force, a power, the energy with which
to transform myself and the world.*

*God's love allows me to let go of all the things I had
been trapped by . . . God's love is a power that liberates
me . . . and as I fill myself with this divine love, I can feel
the power of this growing within myself . . . Peace, love,
truth, joy, purity . . . these are the powers I have received
from the Supreme . . . and as these qualities surface, I can
also feel how they reach right down into the depth, the
core of my being . . . I can feel the power generated within
the soul from the Almighty Authority . . . I receive this
as my inheritance . . . the gift of inner power . . . I can
feel the strength and the fullness of this.*

*In the state of fullness, I know that keeping this
connection with the Supreme, I will be able to deal with
the obstacles and challenges of the world out there . . . the
challenges in relationships, and most of all the challenges
that will come from the traits I carry within myself,
which haven't yet been cleansed . . . I have the faith and
courage to know that through this connection with God
there will be victory in all these situations so that only*

*the goodness will manifest and goodness and truth will
prevail.*

*From the Source of light and might I have received
the understanding of what is true and false . . . My
conscience is awake, alert, refined, and clear . . . and
I can discern how to respond to the people, situations,
and circumstances placed before me . . . God's love has
liberated me from my desires and attachments, and so my
capacity to decide is pristine, accurate . . . I know that as I
follow the instructions of my Supreme Teacher and Guide,
every step will take me closer to my own truth, to my final
destination . . . and every action will be a contribution to
help the world be a better place.*

*In the presence of the Divine, I trust that my thoughts,
my words, and my actions will reflect the special gift of
spiritual power that I have been blessed with, and each
moment will be worthwhile and will make a difference in
the world around me and the world at large . . . God's
light and might reach out across the world . . . and the
darkness ends, the dawn becomes visible, and we move
toward the day . . . a better world for all.*

4 | THE DESTINATION

PREPARATION

An understanding of the self or soul, the soul's relationship with God, and the benefits of the clear and loving connection between the two is central to the meditation journey for which this book is a guide. We have looked at the eternal and nonphysical nature of the soul and the Supreme and at the flow of cognizant energy that occurs when they interact. We have also seen how spiritual power benefits relationships at the human level. Based on the understanding shared so far, we can look in more detail at the method and process of Raja Yoga meditation and see where it can lead us.

Previously, the soul allowed its mind to run free like a wild horse. At times this felt exhilarating, but fear and stubbornness also drove the horse. Sometimes it injured itself or collapsed with exhaustion. Sometimes it hurt others, too. It often became hot and bothered, and its energy was not used to much purpose.

The first step in meditation is to train the mind to move away from the fields that it roams so naturally and easily but that also cause it to become weary and distressed: thoughts of people, situations, all the physical factors of the world. For this, I very consciously use my awareness to relax the body so that my mental energies are no longer locked in it. It then becomes possible to turn those energies inward to the level of eternal truth.

Here is an example of the process:

Sitting comfortably, I take a few deep breaths to allow my body to be energized and at the same time become cool and calm . . . I feel my body settling down . . . I am aware of it as my physical vehicle . . . I take the time to feel its extremities, my fingers, my toes . . . and I let this awareness move through the body, consciously relaxing each part . . .

I become aware of the muscles in my feet, in my legs, my back, my shoulders . . . Keeping my back upright to stay alert, I let go of the tension I have been holding and feel it dissolve . . . I let the tension in my shoulders melt, and my arms relax . . . I become aware of my neck, and tightness drops away . . . I relax the muscles in my face so there is no pressure or strain . . .

With my eyes open, gently ahead, alert but not staring, I come to the forehead . . . My thoughts focus here . . . I can feel light radiating from a source, a spark of life at the center of the forehead . . . This is I, the eternal soul, the

origin of awareness in this physical body . . . I am a soul,
not the body . . . but this body is a wonderful vehicle that
I hold in trust . . . In this awareness of the soul, looking
inward, within this spark of light, I realize that other
beings are also souls, beings of peace.

Going deep inside, my thoughts slow down and I focus on
the point of peace within . . . As my mind becomes calm and
peaceful, I am able to connect with the Supreme, the Being of
Light . . . and God's light and love come shining through.

In this exercise, I am using my knowledge of the soul
and its relationship with the body to rein in the mind and
loosen the grip that the body has on the mind's energies.
I do this gently and carefully, recognizing that the mind
has suffered because of its overidentification with the body
and the rest of the material world.

I need a mixture of kindness and firmness to guide the
mind in the direction of my choice instead of having it race off
again on more unproductive adventures. I want to move it in a
positive direction by focusing its awareness on eternal truth. I
initiate meditation with my intellect, selecting thoughts that
will take the mind in the direction of the soul and God.

CONTEMPLATION

In a second stage, my mind starts to make the connection with the Supreme and begins to feel a flow of positive energy. This can be described as the stage of contemplation. I am reflecting on the different relationships between the soul and the Supreme and on God's qualities and roles. The insights in this book provide food for these thoughts, but it is the feelings and emotions that come when the food is digested and, further, the change in *sanskaras* that bring inner strength and healing.

Contemplation does not require rehearsal of a litany of ideas; rather, it's giving my mind a specific task within whatever time I have allotted for meditation. For example, I may decide I am going to think about God as the being of truth and let my mind explore the truth within God and the truth God shares. As I do so, I'll begin to savor the contentment truth brings.

The purpose of giving myself a theme is to start my meditation in a creative way rather than sitting and waiting for something to happen. It's like telephoning someone: You have to lift the handset, dial the right numbers, and have an idea of what you want to say or hear before getting through. Preparing the body and mind and moving the mind in a specific direction are necessary steps in connecting with God.

Perhaps after a while I'll find my thoughts and feelings moving in a different direction from the one I chose at the outset. That doesn't matter. It will still be a useful meditation as long as I am within the domain of the soul and God. The track I find myself following may be where my greatest need lies right now.

CONCENTRATION

As my mind contemplates aspects of God's truth, it may reach a third stage in the process: that of concentration. Here there is the taste of real stillness and silence as other thoughts subside. The mind is slowing down and working in one direction, toward the being of truth whom we call God, and I am beginning to savor the experience of connecting with God.

Sometimes I'll sit in the meditation and instantly fly into the happiness of this experience without intervening steps. At other times it won't be so easy, but that is when an understanding of the process becomes particularly valuable.

I may find that during the first two stages, meditation and contemplation, many stray thoughts are coming to distract me. That is not surprising, as the mind has been busy with many other concerns. Recognizing this, all I have to do in that moment is tell the mind it can deal with those issues later, but right now I want it to take me to God, the being of light who has so much to offer me.

If I find that although my mind is moving in the right direction, my experience is still only at the level of thinking rather than feeling, that is also okay. It's better to keep the mind occupied in thinking about the soul and the Supreme than in straying uselessly into other areas. In fact, to have come this far is a breakthrough, because relatively few people these days create space for thoughts of the divine.

REALIZATION

Gradually, as I train my mind to keep returning to these thoughts, it will become better able to stay focused. I'll then be in a better position to start experiencing the sweetness of silent communion with the Supreme.

I can create small intervals between thoughts. For example, I may have been contemplating the role of God as my Supreme Mother, listing in my mind the qualities of God as the Mother. If I slow these thoughts and start creating pauses between them, I'll allow the mind to move momentarily into a silence in which there'll be great refreshment.

This is the beginning of the fourth stage: that of realization of truth. Each one's capacity and ability to experience this stage is unique, and it happens in different ways for different individuals. But the essence, however described, is that I feel I am in God's presence and God's qualities are resonating with my own original qualities so that I feel my own fullest potential to be realized. In this experience, the mind comes to a state of absolute stillness, and my *sanskaras*—personality traits—are quiescent. It is not an empty silence but one filled with peace, purity, love, wisdom, and power.

This stage of realization comes as a unified whole: Only

afterward can I put labels on different aspects of it, rather as someone might describe having had a good sleep only when he awakens. There is total absorption in the experience as it happens. Later, I will be able to say yes, I now know what love and truth really mean.

TRANSFORMATION

The longer the periods I spend in the state of realization, the deeper the imprints of these positive attributes will be within me. I am allowing God to influence me, absorbing the benefit of the company of the Supreme.

A stage comes where, having gone through the experience of realization many times, there is such a stock of good thoughts and feelings accumulated that positive *sanskaras* are dominant, and negative tendencies displaced. Then, no matter what external stimulus comes, the response is from these positive *sanskaras*, giving rise to positive thoughts, feelings, and actions.

To achieve this stage, my intellect needs to recognize and accept the power and validity of these ideas and concepts. My mind has to value peace and the insights and experiences that accompany it so highly as to enable it to let go of its previous emotional investment in worldly concerns.

Where I do have continuing responsibilities, I should understand that they will be fulfilled most effectively if I give priority to linking my mind and intellect with God. This is because God is not subject to the selfishness that distorts my own perception.

Seeing the world through God's eyes, as it were, I'm able to act with truth and love, and gradually my own being will become filled with peace, compassion, contentment, and wisdom.

LIFESTYLE

Meditation means changing the direction of my thoughts and disciplining my mind to work in a specific way, focusing on my inner world. The mind is constantly creating thought, and meditation allows me to take charge of that process. The way I live, however, will influence the ease with which I can do this.

Four lifestyle factors that help meditation to develop smoothly are:

1. *Information*: Although silence in the mind can be a powerful stage in meditation, its value lies in the concentrated experience achieved when I have focused my thoughts in the right way. Simply to try to make the mind silent, without proper information, is extremely difficult. Regular spiritual study, reminding me of the purpose of meditation, the knowledge of the self and the Supreme, and the connection of meditation with life, gives the mind the food it needs to grow in the right direction. It protects it against external influences and provides strength for the soul in continuing on its challenging journey.

2. *Practice*: One can know the technique of playing a piano, but without practice, the skill will never come. If I truly want to undertake the journey of meditation, it isn't enough to meditate for a day and then forget about it for a month. Even ten minutes, morning and evening, will make a big difference. But it must be regular. As the benefits become clear to me, I'll be motivated naturally to find more time.

3. *Company*: Everything I see and hear affects my mind and will make a difference to my meditation. I can avoid some of the influences that make it harder for me to focus my thoughts in God's direction. What are the books and magazines I read and the television programs I watch? Powerful images that stimulate the physical senses will take me in the opposite direction from the one I have chosen. Up to a point, I'll be able to choose the people I mix with, too. I want the seedling of truth that has emerged within the soul to grow strong and healthy.

4. *Diet*: There's truth in the saying that we are what we eat. In India, foods are classified on three levels.

Satvic foods, mostly vegetarian, are held to be conductive to peace of mind and nonviolence. A *rajsic* diet, though it may still be vegetarian, is very rich and causes heaviness in mind and body. It includes a lot of butter, cheese, foods fried in oil, and strong spices. *Tamsic* foods, which include meat, fish, and eggs, are held to stimulate the physical senses and the passions. Alcohol and other drugs come into this third category, too. Generally, vegetarian food, cooked in a peaceful atmosphere, will be most helpful to my meditation, whereas nonvegetarian food, especially if prepared in a stress-filled commercial setting, will affect my mind adversely. It's good for people interested in meditation to be aware of these factors so that when practicable, they can experiment with changes and judge for themselves the impact on mind and body.

PURE MOTIVES

Purity of motive is the key that will unlock a better future. The selfishness that accompanied body-consciousness caused cycles of action and reaction that made our lives increasingly stressful. When I maintain my link of love with God, God's truth and love change my understanding of the purpose of life and inform my actions from a perspective of giving rather than taking.

When I act for the love of God, those actions deepen my connection with God. A beneficial cycle of positive action and reaction gets under way that is a healing antidote to the harsh pressures of modern living.

When I begin to meditate, I get to know my strengths and weaknesses. I rediscover my own inner beauty, but I also start to learn how fickle and deceptive my mind can be. I also discover that it is possible to train and channel this energy called the mind, giving it purpose and power.

As I continue to meditate, I learn to make my mind calm and peaceful. Hurt feelings are soothed, and old wounds healed. My self-respect grows, and I'm no longer so reactive toward difficult people or situations. I find how valuable it is to maintain a positive attitude and vision toward myself, other people, and life and how damaging it is to use the force of negative feelings and emotions such as criticism and anger. Negativity may win me short-term advantage, but afterward I'll feel guilty or unhappy and burdened by other people's resentment toward me.

I acquire mastery of my feelings and emotions. I develop the practice of pausing at times of difficult decisions to check internally what I should do or say. In such moments, I listen to my higher consciousness, of which God is an unending wellspring, the source of the positive energy that brings lasting solutions, and the closer I get to that, the more accurate my decisions will be.

I also take time to explore my feelings and motives in meditation, cleaning them out to make them positive and strong. I see my weaknesses more clearly, but I don't feel discouraged because I know that they are not original to my nature and that they will fall away as I continue building positive aspects of my character on the path of spirituality. Meditation liberates me from my addictions, whether to substances or to the negative patterns of thought and feeling that trapped me.

Through the power of concentration, I develop many virtues, such as patience, tolerance, sweetness, humility, clarity, determination, and enthusiasm. These strengths start to bring success in the tasks I undertake, where previously there may have been friction and failure. I learn to value myself, love myself, and be able to share the gifts I have received with others.

LEARNING TO GIVE

Meditation opens the door for me to take my inheritance from God. I discover the vastness of the attributes of God, the absolute beauty of the being who is God, and I begin to appreciate that as a child of God, I am entitled to receive God's virtues, powers, and wisdom if I so choose. For that, I need to allow God to come into the heart of my life.

Meditation shows me how I can have God's companionship, protection, blessings, support, guidance, and, most important of all, love. The more I benefit from this perfect relationship, the easier it is for me to drop weak tendencies and create a character filled with newness and strength.

I become a giver instead of a taker or complainer. I accept responsibility for myself instead of waiting for other people, or fate, or God to do something for me. I will do what I need to do and give others the space to do whatever they feel is right without imposing on them.

I become able to see all around me as my spiritual brothers, sensing my connectedness with the vast family of humanity and how we need to know and appreciate each other. Meditation teaches me to see their qualities and to be able to respond to and work with the goodness in others.

Full in my own being, I am able to have good feelings toward others without selfish needs or agendas prejudicing my view. If conflict does arise, meditation will show me how to deal with it and repair any damage.

I become able to bring benefit to others, to serve with genuine altruism, because I am motivated by the experience of God's love rather than by a desire for praise, recognition, or control over others. Actually, when I act in this way, it is still for my own benefit, because it becomes my joy and satisfaction in life to do what God wants of me. Meditation makes me aware that through me, the power of the Divine is able to remove suffering.

Help can be directed to areas of specific need. For example, if a relative or friend is sick, I can draw on God's love to help healing thoughts reach that person. However, I'll be very clear in my mind that it is God's healing power that she needs. If I start seeking to heal others directly, complications may arise that will break my own connection with God.

> *Sitting quietly, I bring my thoughts back to the identity*
> *of my spiritual consciousness . . . I am peace, I am light,*
> *I am a soul . . . I connect with the Supreme, the infinite*
> *spark of light, radiating infinite light . . . God's light*

reaches me . . . I feel filled with light and love . . .
I remember those who are in need and hold them in God's
light . . . God's light and love reach these souls . . .
I surrender them to the Supreme . . . I allow them to
stay in God's light . . . I step out of the way, knowing
God is responsible . . . Staying in God's remembrance,
I let God look after them . . . and God's love surrounds
them, strengthens them, heals them, supports them . . .
I stay in remembrance of One.

Similarly, my thoughts of God can help people in distress
because of external circumstances such as the strife of war or
the suffering accompanying natural disasters.

Sitting quietly, I look at the conditions of the world around
me . . . It seems to be a world in much darkness . . . I
wonder how I can help . . . I see the value of physical
support but also of God's light and love to bring hope for
the future . . . I let my thoughts go beyond the physical
dimension . . . I reach a place of infinite light, a place
of peace . . . Here, in my home, which is also the home of
my Supreme Parent, I feel God's love strengthening me,
making me whole.

God, the Ocean of Love, sends out waves of love that surround me . . . and these waves of love extend to the whole world, reaching souls who have lost hope . . . They feel touched by God's love, and hope reawakens and God's love brings light so they can see a way through the darkness . . . God's love empowers them . . . Courage is born again, and they move toward the light . . . God's love heals them so they can forgive, let go, and move on . . . God's love guides them so they can understand what needs to be done . . . God's love uplifts them and gives them a fresh start . . . The light of God's love removes the darkness and fills the universe until a new dawn begins.

HELPING THE WORLD

Meditation makes me more accepting and tolerant of quirks in personality and behavior, because it lets me see the wider picture within which those quirks arose. It makes me humble and flexible so that I become easier to live with. It does not make me a doormat, but it gives me the inner strength and dignity that enables me to give respect to others and to serve.

Meditation shows me what I have to do for the world. It's not so much my actions as the thought behind them that counts. I do need to act, but it is the purity and goodness in my actions that will make the world a better place. God gives me the strength to act in this way, with pure motivation.

Meditation teaches me a life of simplicity so that I am not draining the earth of its limited natural resources. I learn how to use my own resources, including both physical and spiritual assets, in a worthwhile way. As my link with God deepens, I feel I am earning a huge fortune in the spiritual sense, recovering my purity, creative power, and contentment. I sense that unlike physical wealth, this is a fortune that will last into eternity.

People often ask, How can meditation help the world? They feel that political action, aimed at economic justice, offers the best chance for change. It is interesting, however, that since the mid-1980s, the United Nations has been promoting the recognition that for a better world we need not just development in the economic sense but human development, too.

We have been through a period in which we tended to forget about values at the human level. Material values dominated our decision making, both personal and political. Even when we recognized the importance of deeper values, we lacked the power to live by them. Someone might declare that she values truth, for example, but if this becomes mere words rather than a message lived in action and reality, it will lack authority and will be ignored.

Meditation gives me the power to follow a path of truth. It brings out shared aspects of human consciousness that are deep and true but became submerged beneath more shallow concerns. It enables me to become a better person and to contribute that quality to human affairs. As people change in this way and come back to living by higher values, we can expect social structures and systems to change in that direction too, because it is human consciousness that gives rise to these systems.

My experience of God through meditation and the purification that occurs through this connection automatically serve the world around me as the quality of my thoughts, words, actions, and vibrations improves.

Among all the world's troubles, one that is perhaps recognized as the most catastrophic is the destruction of the earth's ecosystem. When human consciousness became separated from God, a process began in which we progressively lost respect for ourselves and the world around us.

We have been exploiting and violating nature, destroying the fragile ecosystem that supports life, and today there is a question about the future of the planet. Many feel helpless in the face of the forces that seem to be sweeping us further toward disaster.

Through meditation, we can help bring about renewal in nature. The problems are so great that it might seem our thoughts could never be more than a drop in an ocean. However, human consciousness created the destructive forces, and now God needs us to align our consciousness with divine truth to restore order.

> *The awareness of I, the soul, my thoughts, turn to the Supreme, my compassionate Mother, my loving Father . . . God's love and purity reach the soul . . . Both are renewed, touched by God's pure rays of light . . . As I,*

*the soul, stay connected with the Supreme, God's peace
reaches out into the universe . . . Its soothing touch embraces
the elements, taking away the heat, compensating for the
violence and aggression inflicted . . . Peace returns to the
planet itself . . . The warmth of God's love claims the
waters and skies and all forms of life.*

*Recognizing how much I have been sustained by the earth,
I see it is time for the planet to be restored to its own true
state through rays of divine love, purity, and peace . . .
and as the earth is cleansed and serenity and harmony
return to the elements, chaos subsides . . . The planet
recovers its original, fresh, beautiful state . . . With soul
and matter working together in harmony, nature again
cooperates, offering her comforts, fruits, and love.*

GOD'S FORGIVENESS

One very personal experience is of how meditation enables me to feel God's forgiveness as well as His love and support. The sorrow that I have caused to others and the imprints left on my own being through my wrong actions are accounts that need to be settled.

When I sit in meditation and feel God's love, I am able to realize the mistakes I have made and the lessons I need to learn. Realization, honesty, and humility allow me to draw on so much of God's positive power that I can settle the accounts of the past comfortably, without pain or a sense of punishment.

It is as though God takes responsibility for the past and removes all traces of the rubbish I had accumulated within me.

God's love cleanses me, purifies me, and reforms me. It frees me from the complications created by my past mistakes so that they no longer block my progress toward my own perfection as a human being.

YOGA POWER

The power of positive thought works at an immediate, visible level. As it is brought into focus by meditation, it reflects on my face and through my physical presence and translates into words and actions. Thus, each day, the meditation I practice helps me manage my life, facilitating balanced decision making, good relationships and interactions, and better health.

I know that within my personality there is a mixture of positive and negative tendencies. Meditation replenishes my natural qualities of peace, goodwill, and happiness, creating a store of benevolent energy, the result of the connection with God. When expressed, this energy is called yoga power. It gives me the strength to continue to reinforce the positive, wise, and good in my character and quietly let go of that which is not so good. The benefits for mind, body, and relationships are immediate.

Yoga power is pure consciousness accumulated through loving remembrance of God. It protects me from negative influences, both inner and outer. It ensures that when I'm faced with negativity in others or with a negative atmosphere, there aren't negative responses triggered within me.

I stay protected by God's light and truth, and my responses are filled with that power.

Meditation gives me the courage to engage with the world on a wider basis than meeting my own or my immediate family's needs. It gives me independence of spirit, enabling me to use my time and energy and other resources for the wider good while also sustaining those close to me.

THE LIFE OF A YOGI

Beyond these immediate practical benefits, yoga becomes a conscious choice in the style of life I follow so that the relationship with God unfolds with increasing depth, intimacy, and beauty.

As this process continues, the journey becomes ever more rich, varied, and challenging, like the increasing levels of difficulty in an adventure game. The monsters I meet are nothing more than dark spots within my own psyche, and the situations that come to face me are obstacles of my own creation. When I stay true to God with faith and obedience, holding fast to the pure consciousness of the Supreme, I'll find difficulties that looked like mountains shrinking into mustard seeds.

The times when I'll shake are those when I don't immediately realize that the obstacles have been created by aspects of my own personality. At such times, I'll project the problem outside of me. It will seem so clear to me that other people or intolerable circumstances are to blame! I'll find all sorts of reasons to justify my predicament.

Through meditating every day and staying connected to the Supreme, I avoid this trap. God's pure vision toward me enables me to face the fact that the obstacles are a reflection of my weakness and deficiencies. Then, if I respond positively, not with self-criticism but by paying more attention to yoga, God will make good the weakness and fill in the deficiencies. As if by magic, the obstacles disappear.

The power of yoga, which is also the power of God's love, dissolves difficulties. As I experiment with this and see the fruits in my life, my trust in God deepens and my self-confidence grows. I learn from each situation that comes and move forward to a higher level.

The relationship with God becomes constant, natural, and easy, and the power that flows from it shapes everything I do. In the joy of knowing myself as a child of God, I wish only to live by my Father's highest standards, keeping God in my heart to guide me. In this state of natural connection, I feel myself to be the worthy child of this highest of all parents.

I am also aware that the Supreme Teacher is sharing the most valuable wisdom with me and that as I grasp the truth and reflect it through my actions, my life is becoming an inspiration for others.

The life of a yogi is different from the experiences others have of the world. I am still within the world, but when I am experiencing the union with God, I show lightness, easiness, and stability as my journey continues. I sail through waves of fame or damnation, fortune or defeat, with equanimity.

A yogi maintains the original qualities of the soul and radiates them continually: peace that is undisturbed, love that is unbroken, joy that is unshakable, purity that is unchanging, and truth that is unblemished. These qualities become an attraction for others, too, so that they are inspired to draw closer to God, and the yogi becomes an instrument for spreading God's love and truth to all.

B. K.
JAYANTI

THE DESTINATION

Ultimately, a yogi lives in the world yet is not of the world. This detached yet loving consciousness allows the yogi to live—like an angel—at God's right hand, going beyond the normal limits of matter, beyond tiredness and even old age.

The heart of the yogi has such compassion as to be like a fountain, endlessly sharing treasures from God, generous and open, not seeking a return or imposing any conditions. A yogi is beyond the accounts of giving and taking, acting and reacting, at the human level, so that although the physical body will age, the spirit continues to serve. Most of all, a yogi serves through the vibrations of his being.

Every thought each of us creates, as well as the words we speak and the actions we perform, produces a ripple effect on other people and even on physical surroundings. These vibrations are not physical—they have to do with the consciousness or meaning behind the thought, word, or action. When there is purity of intention, a positive transfer takes place, conveying love and truth. When there is negativity, it is as though we seek to rob others of this same subtle currency.

Even in stillness, whatever I am, as I am, my character sends out vibrations. A yogi, in constant relationship with

God, having completed the journey in which mind, intellect, *sanskaras*, feelings, and emotions are cleansed, emits vibrations of purity in all directions. A yogi doesn't need to speak to be able to serve. A yogi serves simply by being in that state of purity. The vibrations of purity reach others and inspire and empower them by reminding them of their own original truth.

The vibrations of a yogi cleanse the atmosphere of the places where he lives and moves, restoring calm where there has been strife, coolness and reason where there has been confusion. In his complete surrender to God, the yogi becomes an instrument to serve in ways he is not even conscious of, with God's light and God's message of truth and love reaching through him to places of need far across the world.

This is my destination, as a yogi: to be in this world yet free from its limitations—to enjoy a state of such unchanging truth, through union with my Supreme Father, as to have total benevolence. This ideal state becomes possible when God has cleansed my consciousness to the extent that I am able to be a reflection of the Supreme.

Human beings are not created full of flaws. The expression in the Scriptures, that God created us in His own image, is true. It is the destination of all of us to reflect the beauty of the Creator again. It has to happen, because the journey we are taking ultimately returns us to our starting point. We go back to a future in which we live by the pure truth that was ours at the beginning.

ABOUT THE AUTHOR

B.K. Jayanti is a world-renowned teacher of meditation.
She is the European Director of the Brahma Kumaris World
Spiritual University, an international organization working
for world peace through personal transformation.